# HIROSHIGE

*Prints Remastered One*

## GARY LEE KVAMME

Volume 1

Japanese Art Series

Copyright © 2017 by Gary Lee Kvamme
All rights reserved.
Published September 2017

# HIROSHIGE
*Prints Remastered One*

Hiroshige, with the simple and restricted means of the Japanese color-painter and a direct audacity of technique surprising to analyze, carried the natural aspect of old Japan to live before our eyes forever. His devotion to landscape more single and his realistic process greater than that of others.

Hiroshige's sole teacher was nature. He was an arch-impressionist. In special atmospheric effects, such as moonlight, snow, mist and rain, he achieved a variety of effects that were unrivaled at the time. His work had a profound influence on the Impressionists and Post-Impressionists of Europe: Toulouse-Lautrec was fascinated with Hiroshige's daring diagonal compositions and inventive use of perspective, Van Gogh literally copied two prints from Hiroshige's famed series, *100 Famous Views of Edo* in oil paint.

In 1858, at the age of 61, Hiroshige passed away as a result of the Edo cholera epidemic.

Today we have come to estimate Hiroshige's designs for woodblock prints at their true worth and to realize how splendid they are in all the essential qualities that every work of art should have.

Utilizing the Kvamme process of digital enhancement, the tired, timeworn woodblock prints by Hiroshige (1797-1858) are, in the present undertaking, painstakingly restored and re-energized with a vivid and palpable sense of their original freshness and immediacy.

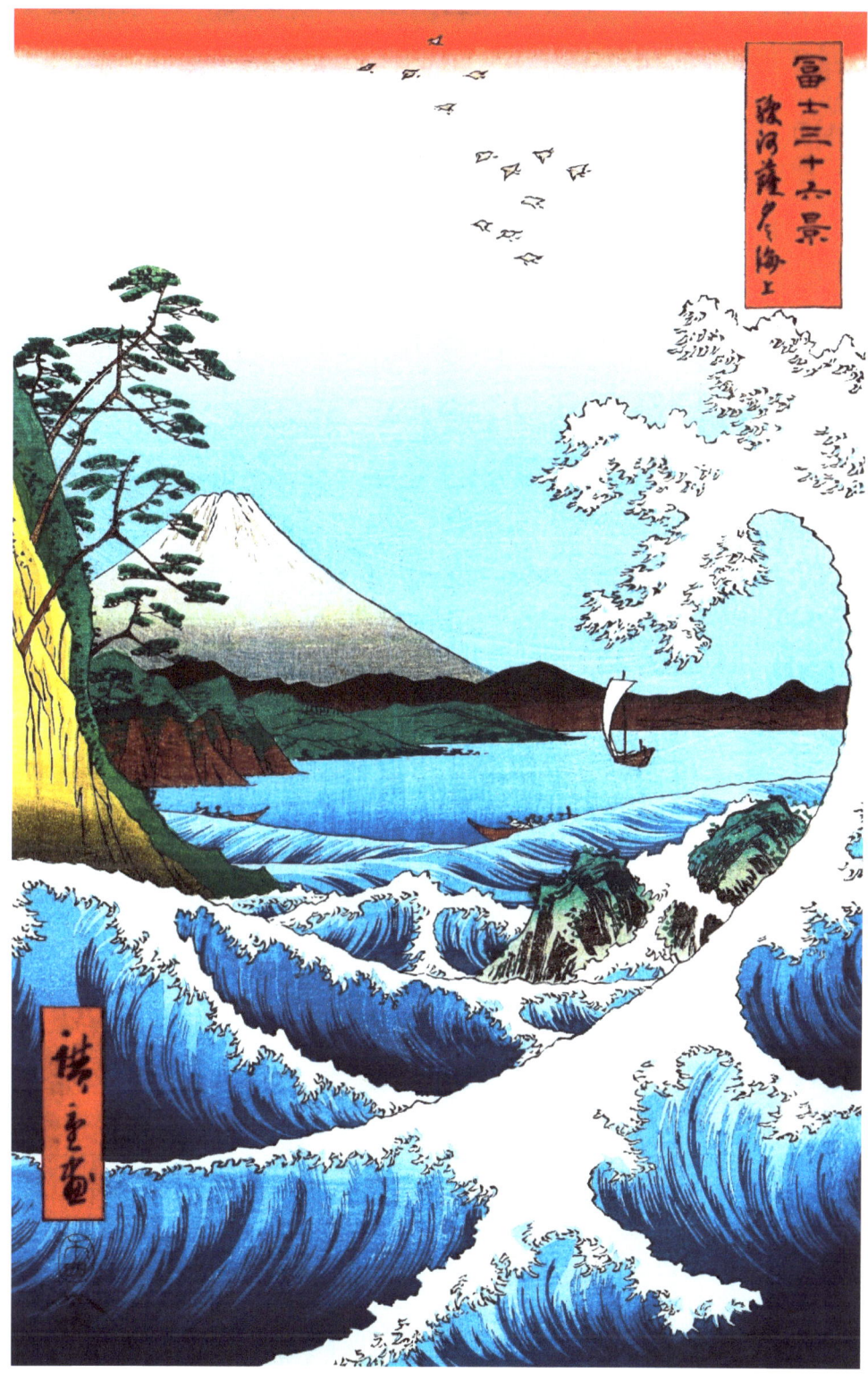

Suruga Satta no kaijō.

A view of Mount Fuji from Satta Point in the Suruga Bay, with breaking waves in the foreground.

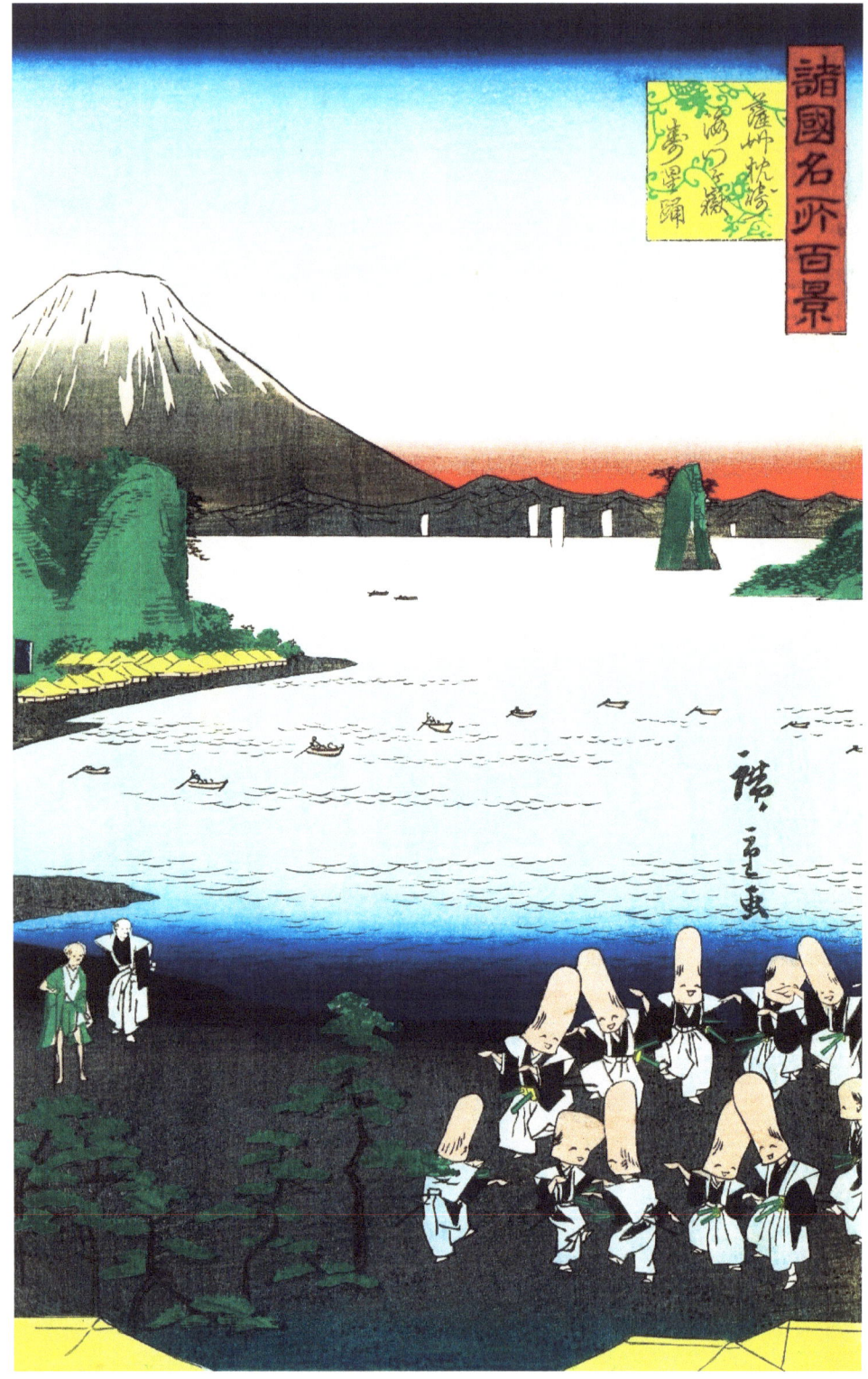

Sasshu makurazaki kaimongadake jusei odori.

A group of dancers wearing oversized masks dancing in a circle on a beach with small village on the shore and a view of snowcapped mountain in the background.

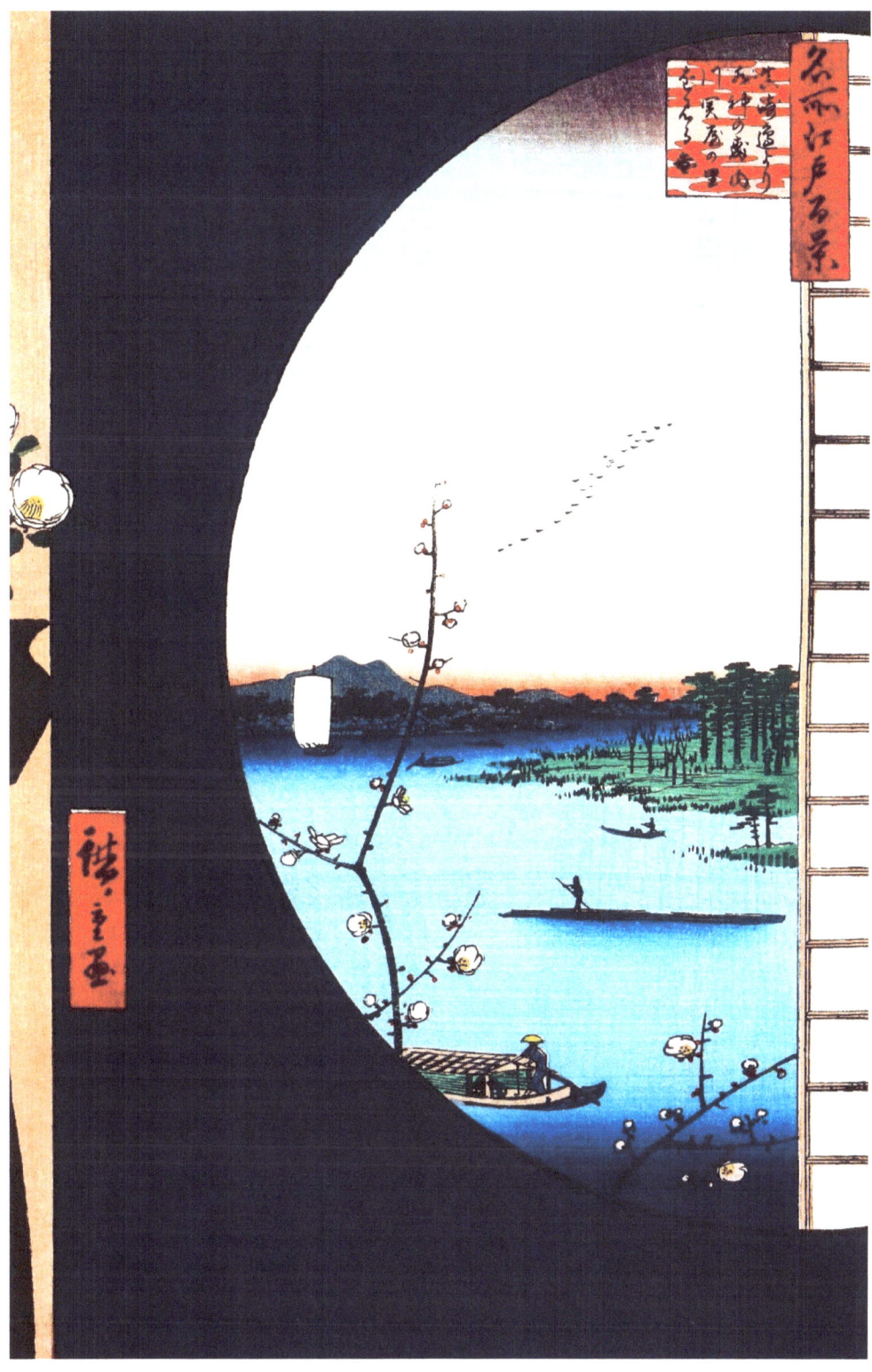

Massaki-hen yori Suijin no mori uchigawa sekiya no sato o miru zu.

A view through a semi-circle of boats on the Uchi River inlet, with blossoms in the foreground and distant view of the Suijin shrine.

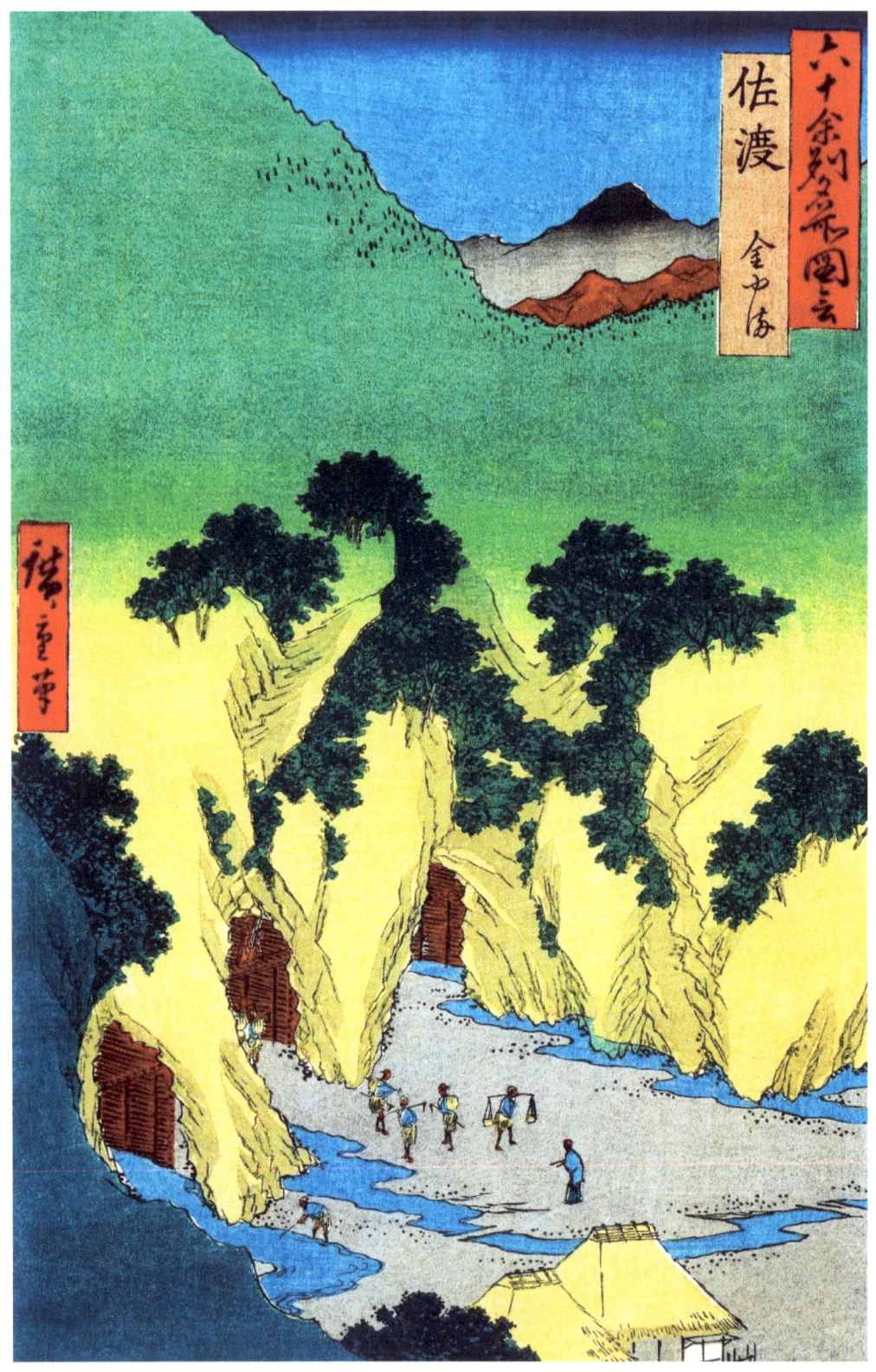

Sado.

Gold mines in cliffs on Sado Island, with miners carrying gold out of the mines.

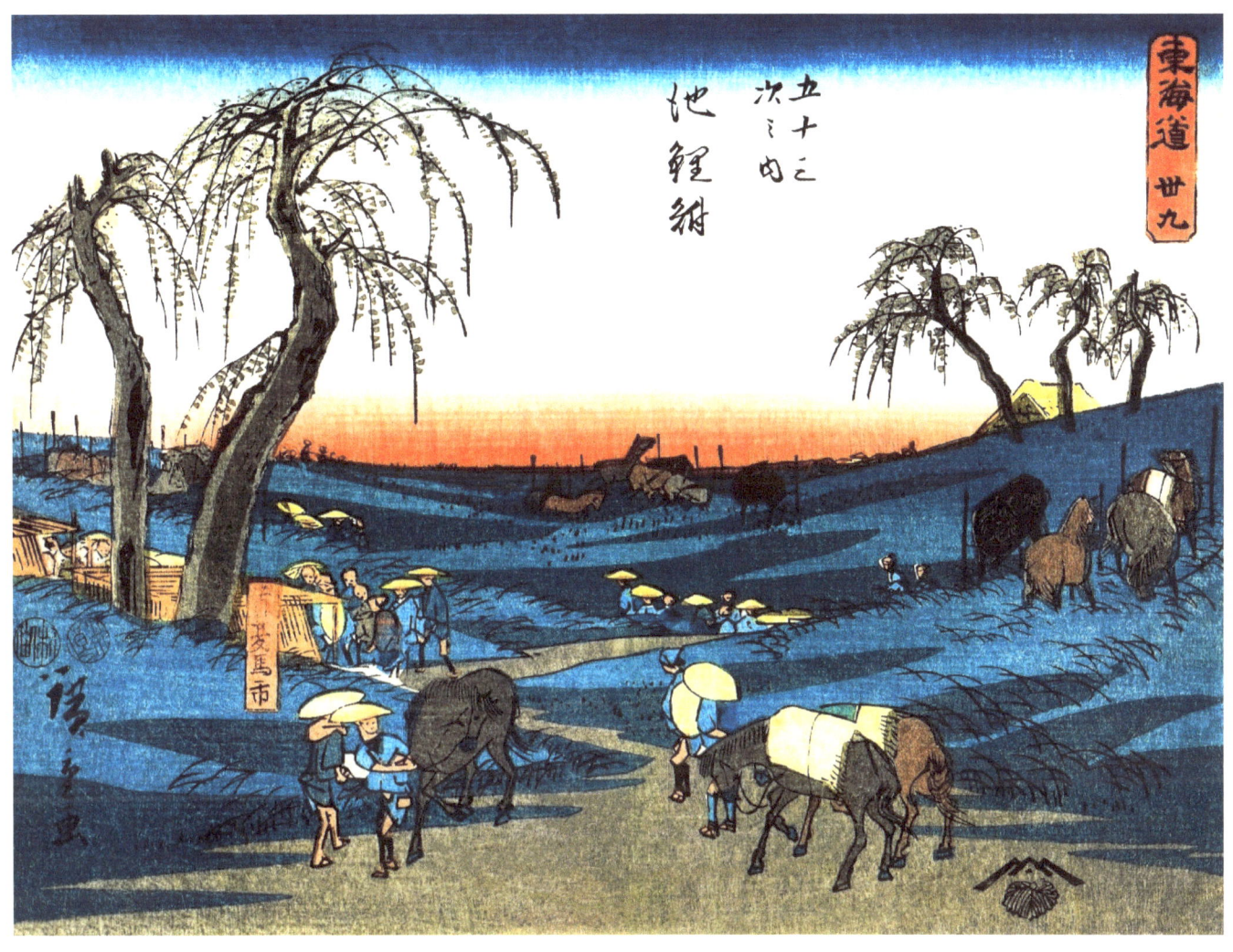

Chiryū.

Travelers leading horses and letting them graze in fields at the Chiryū station on the Tōkaidō Road.

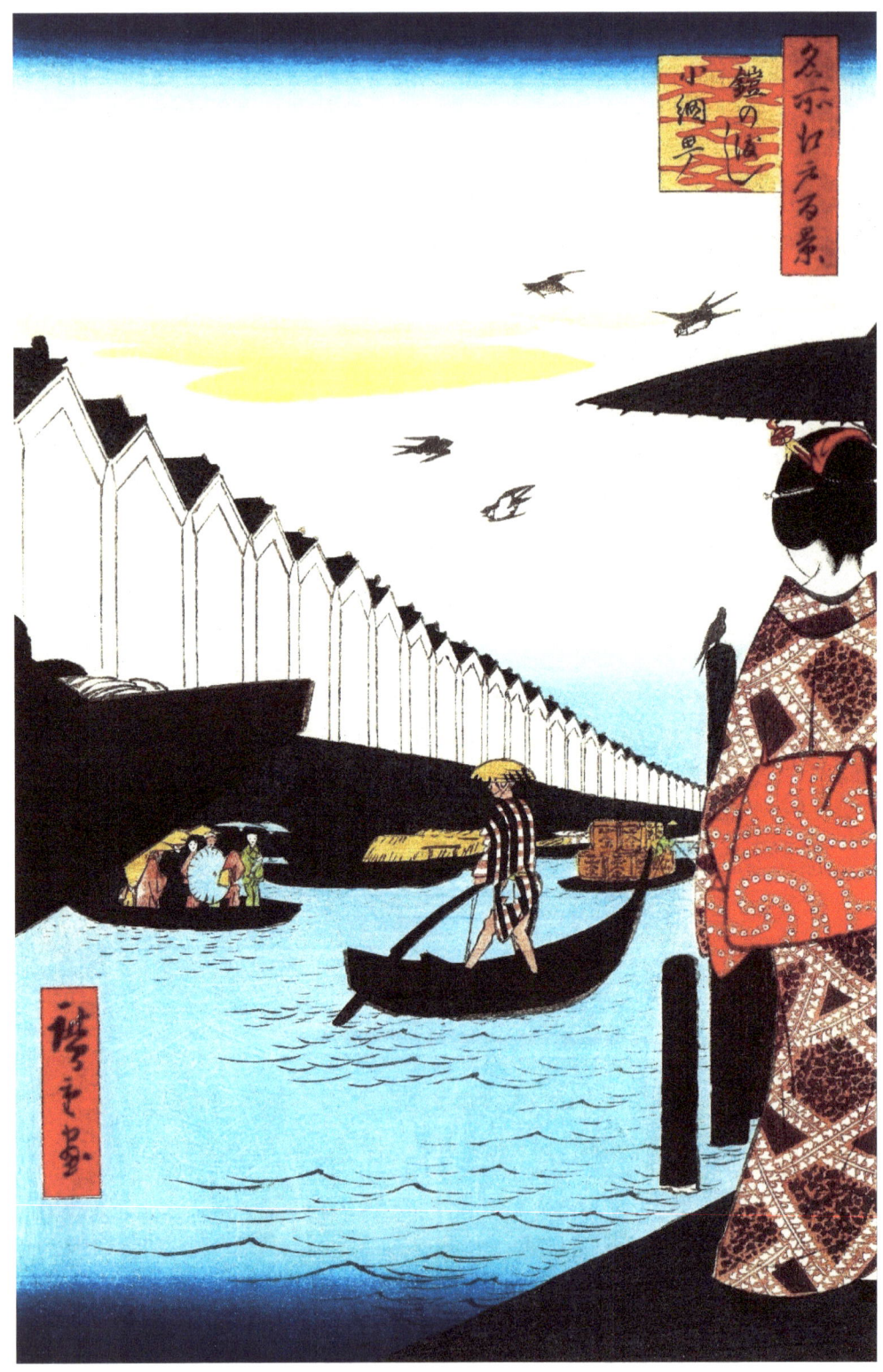

Yoroi-no watashi koami-chō.

A boat ferrying people across a channel while another boat is rowed by a man and several boats in the background are laden with goods; a woman stands along the waterfront.

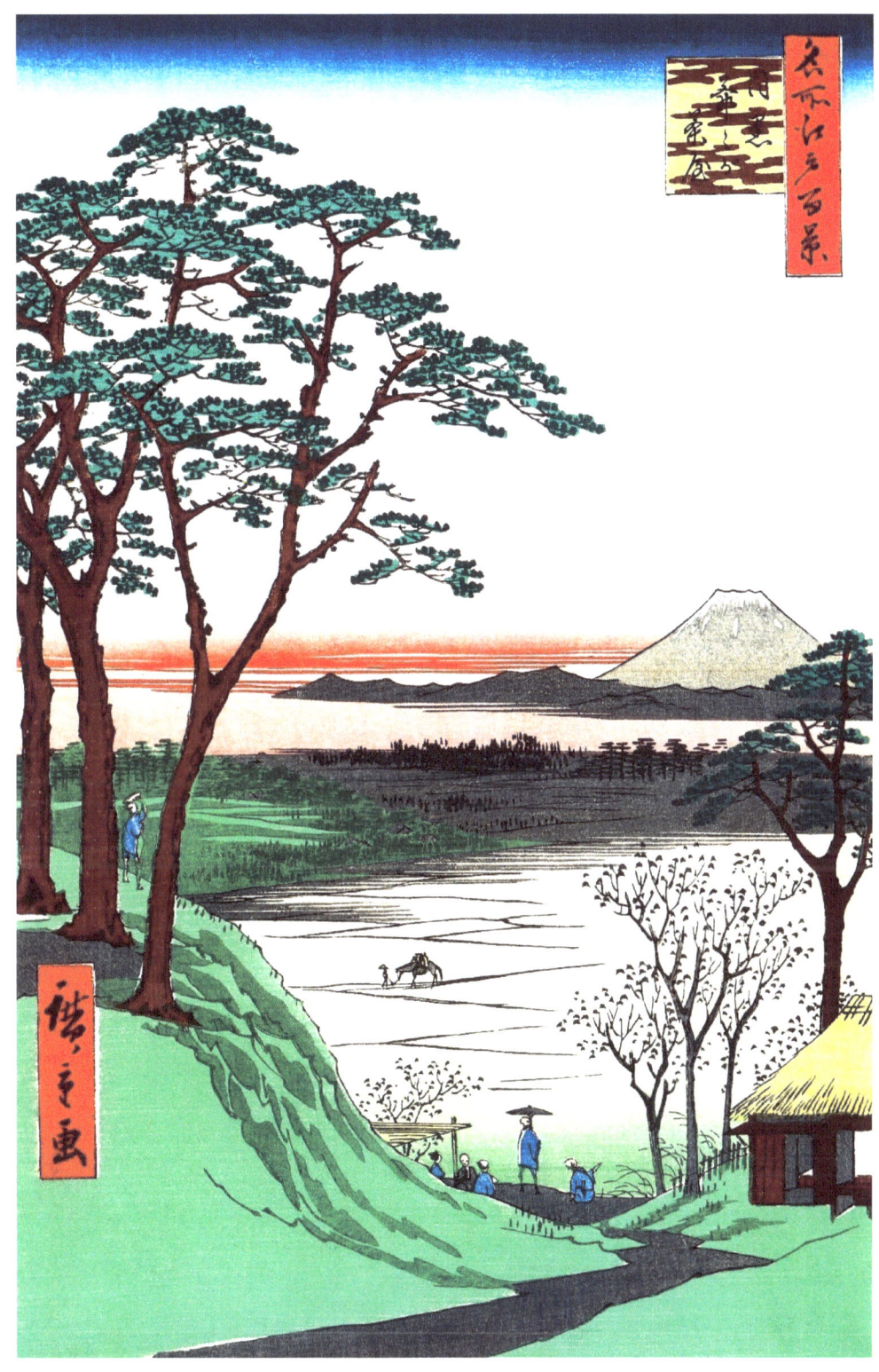

Meguro jijigachaya.

Travelers on roadway near a small teahouse at rest stop, with tall pine trees on the left and view of Mount Fuji in the distance.

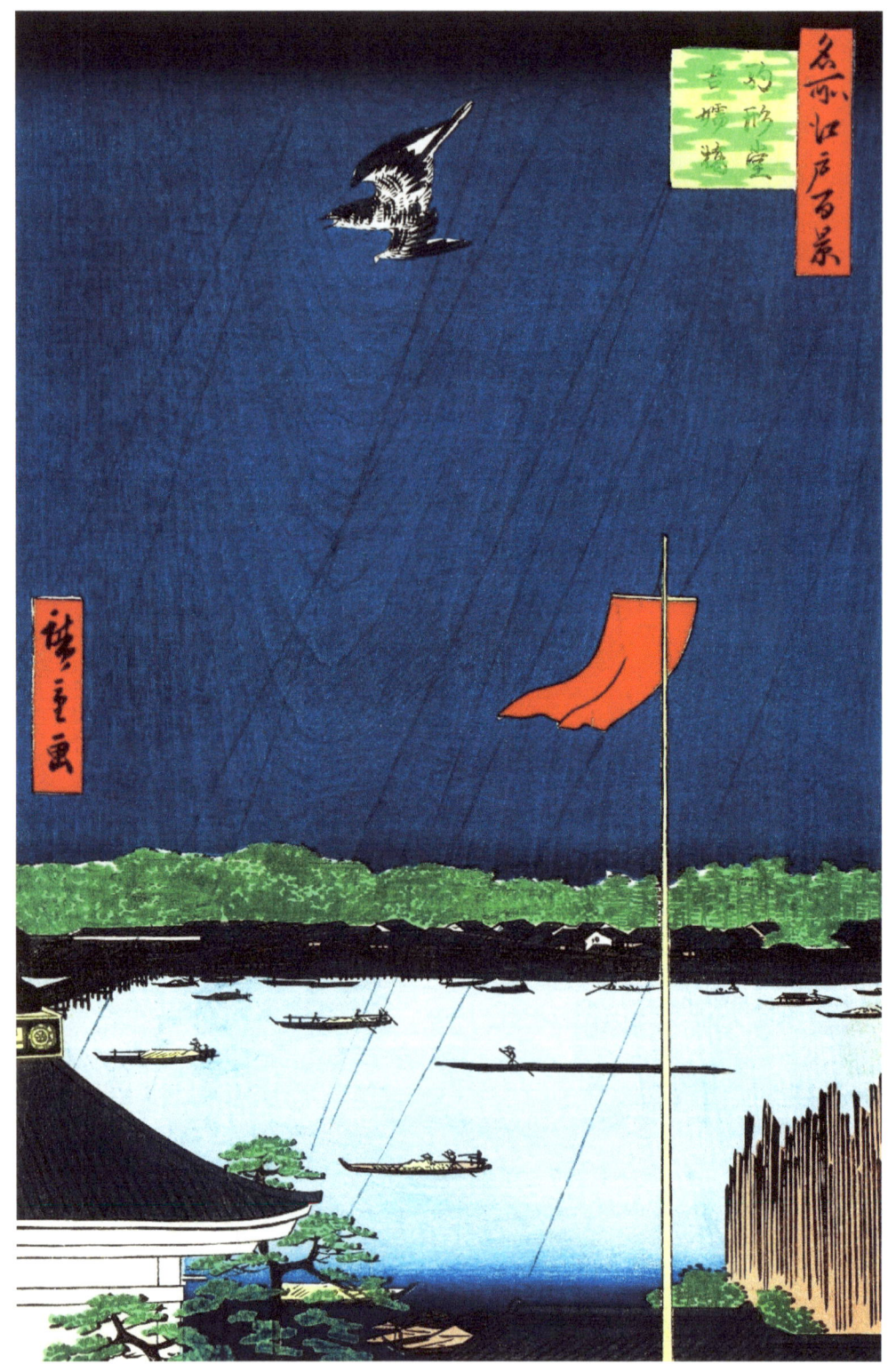

Komagatadō azumabashi.

A bird flying over a river with many boats approaching the Azuma bridge, and the temple in the lower left.

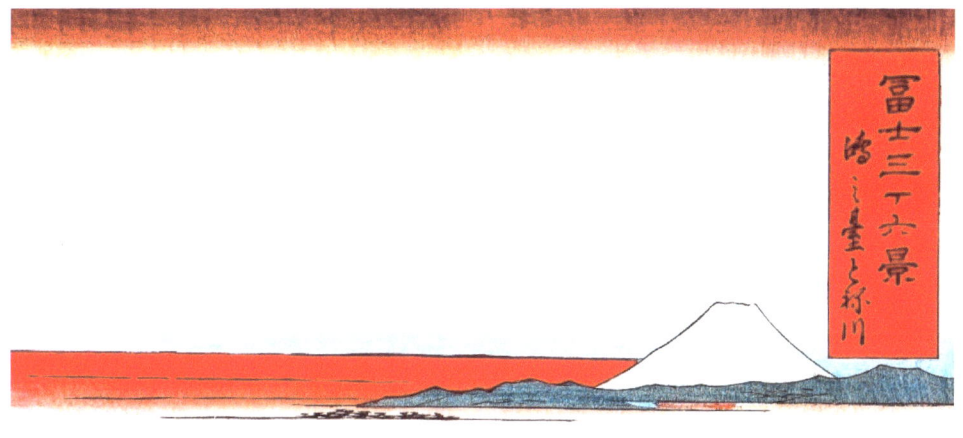

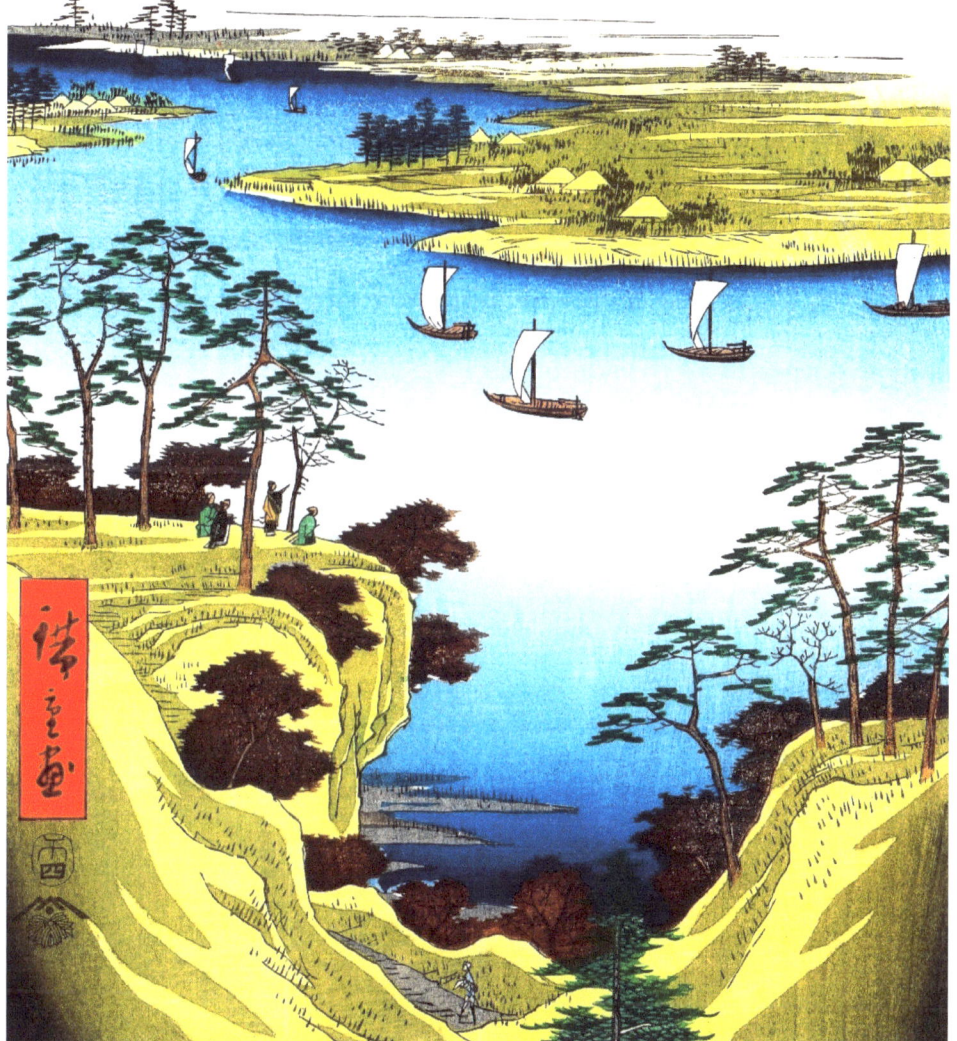

Kōnodai tonegawa.

Sightseers standing on cliff overlooking the Tone River with sailboats and a view of Mount Fuji in the background.

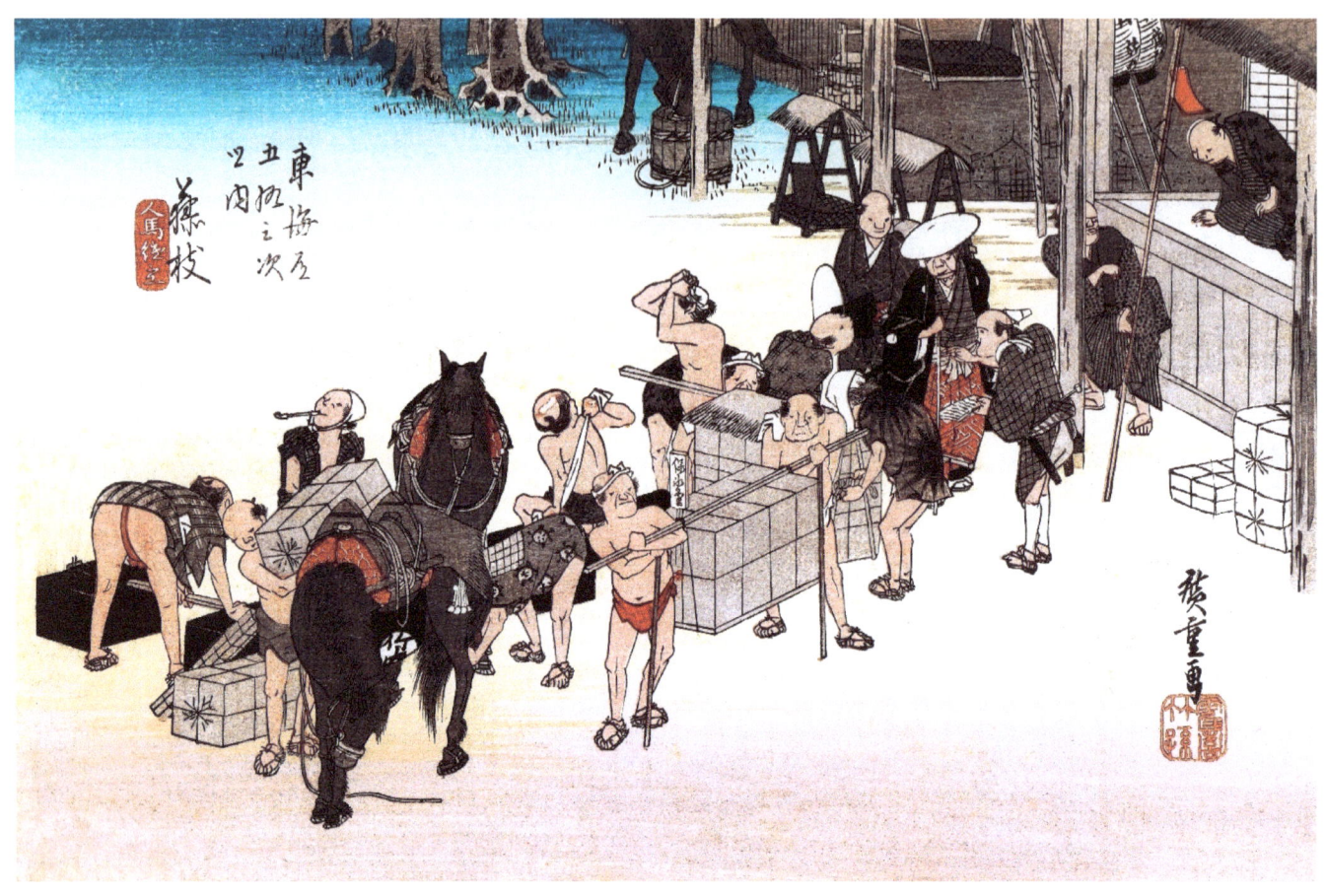

Fujieda.

Travelers with two horses and porters at a rest stop at the Fujieda station on the Tōkaidō Road.

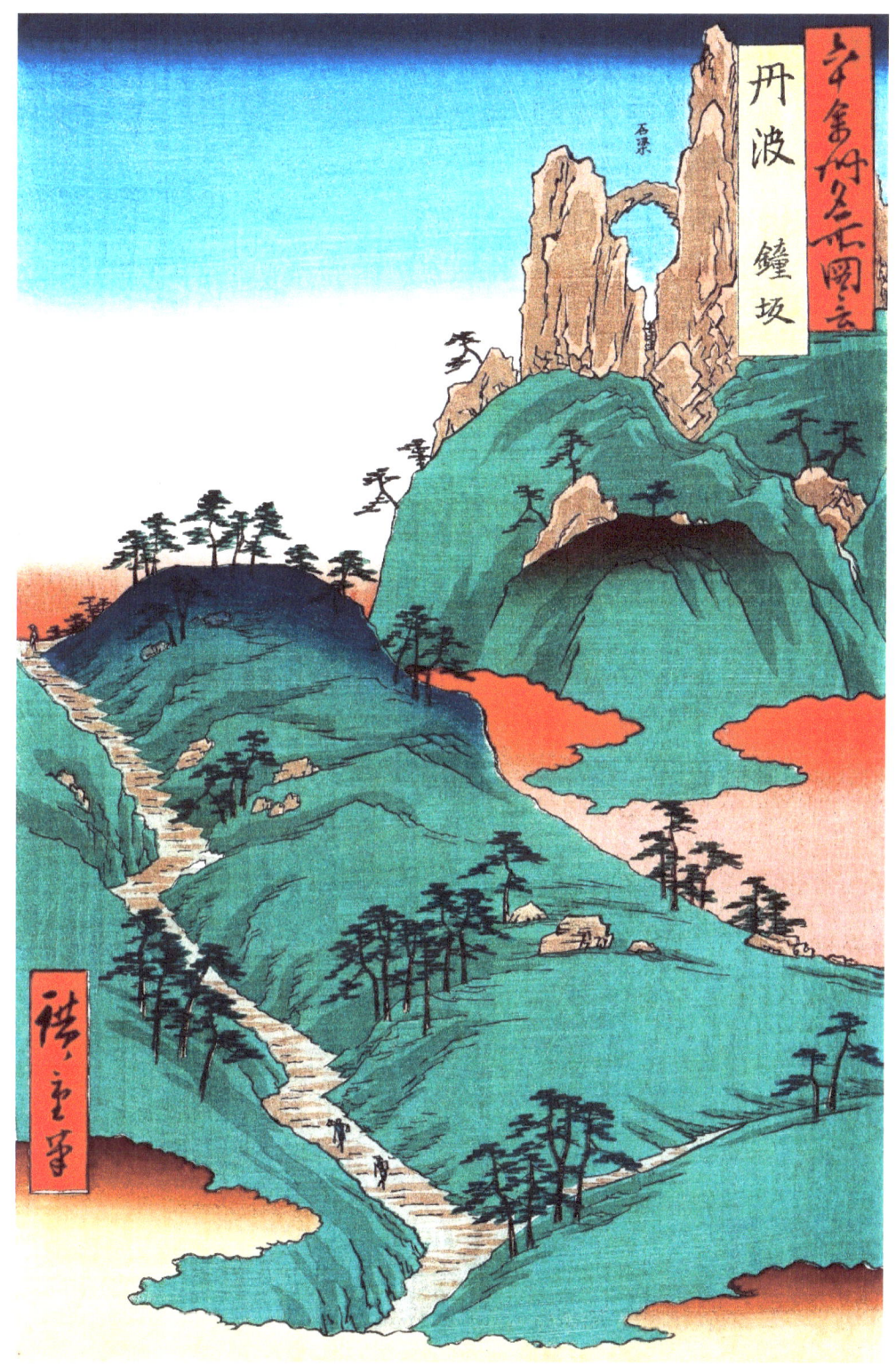

Tanba kanesaka.

A steep landscape rising to a natural bridge of rocks at upper right, with small figures on path in foreground. In the former province called Tanba.

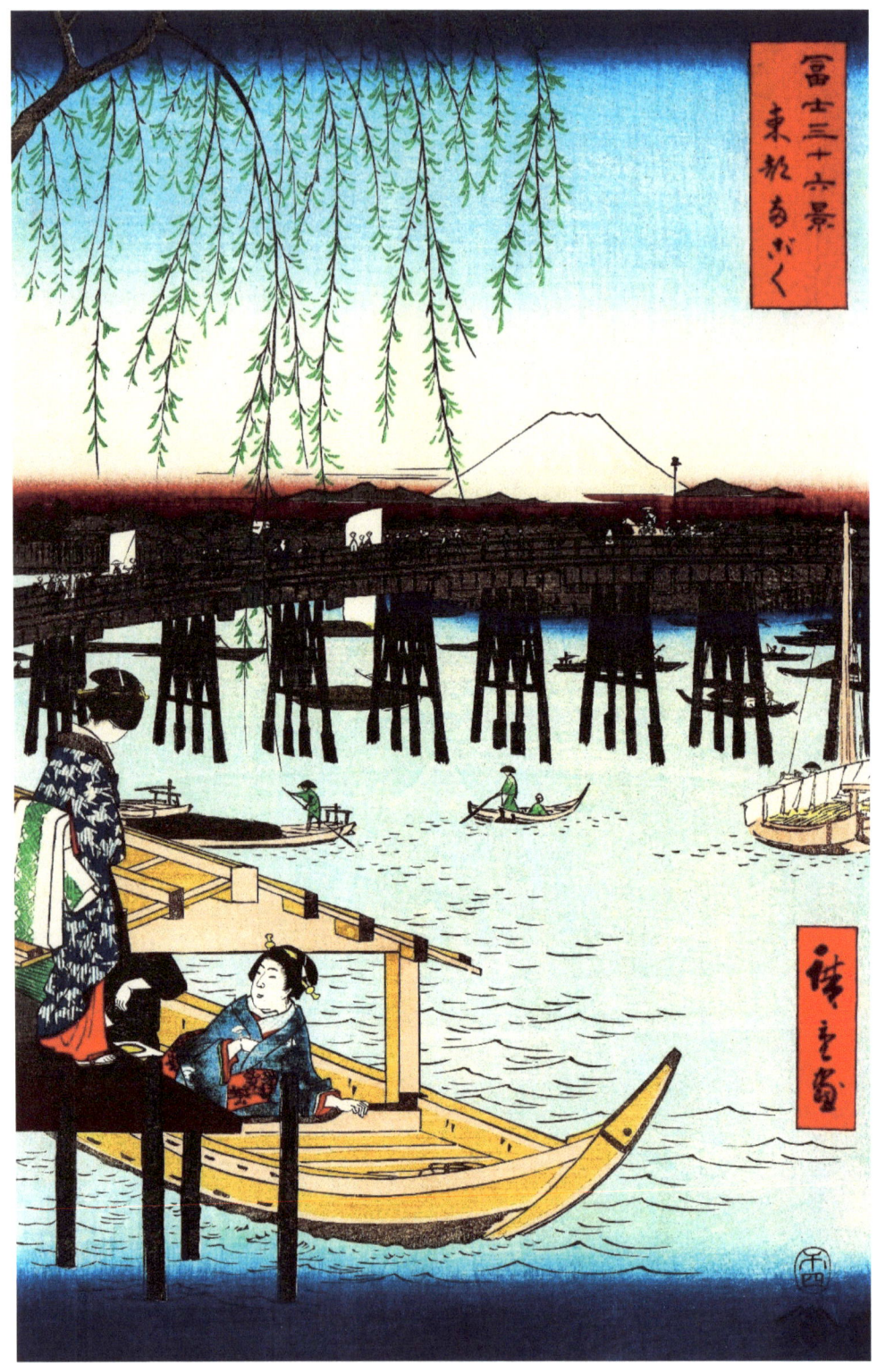

Tōto ryōgoku.

A woman in a boat and a woman standing on a dock, pedestrians crossing a wooden bridge in the middle distance, and a view of Mount Fuji in the background.

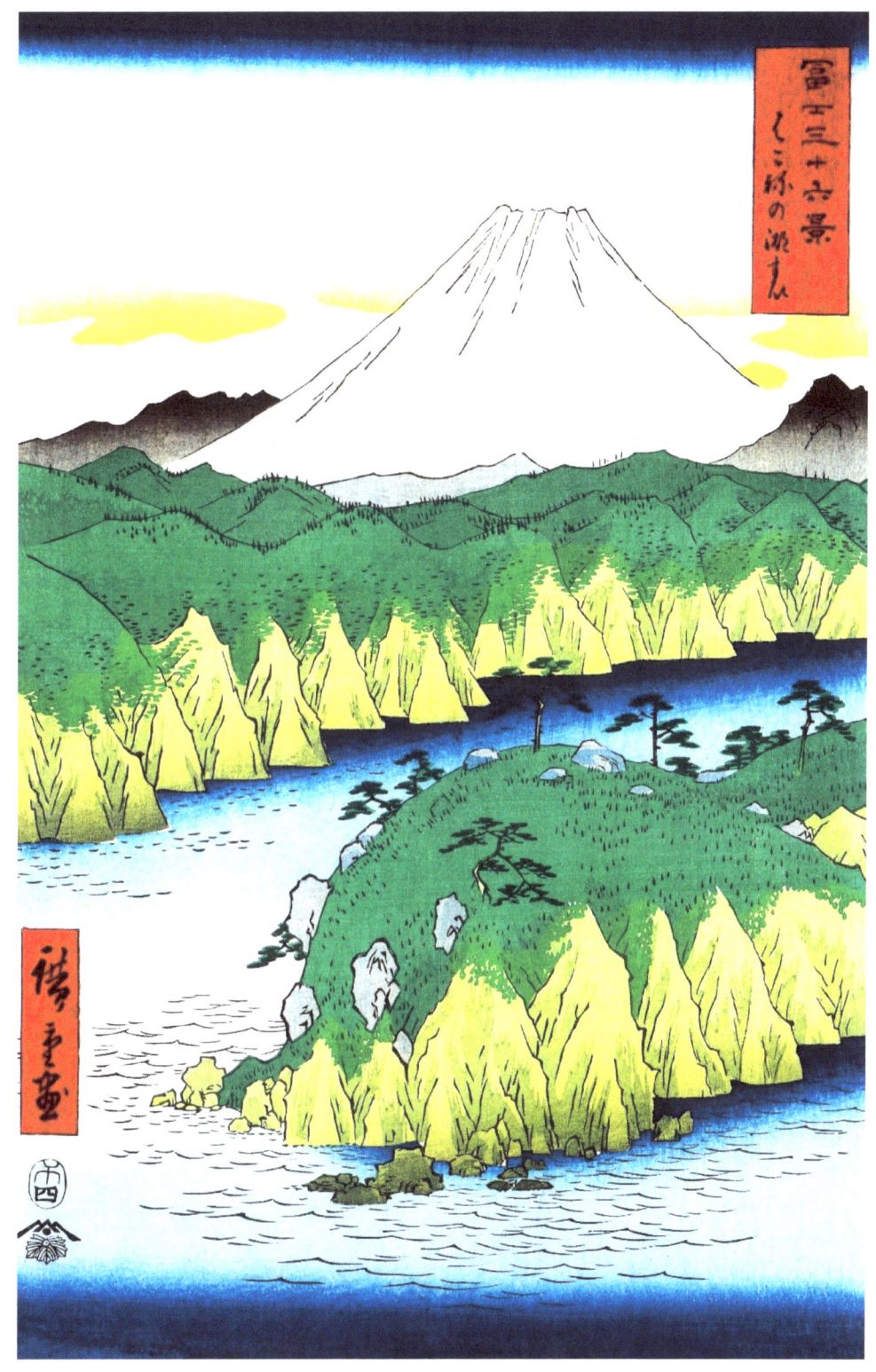

Hakone no kosui.

The steep cliffs and rock formations in Lake Hakone, with a view of Mount Fuji in the background.

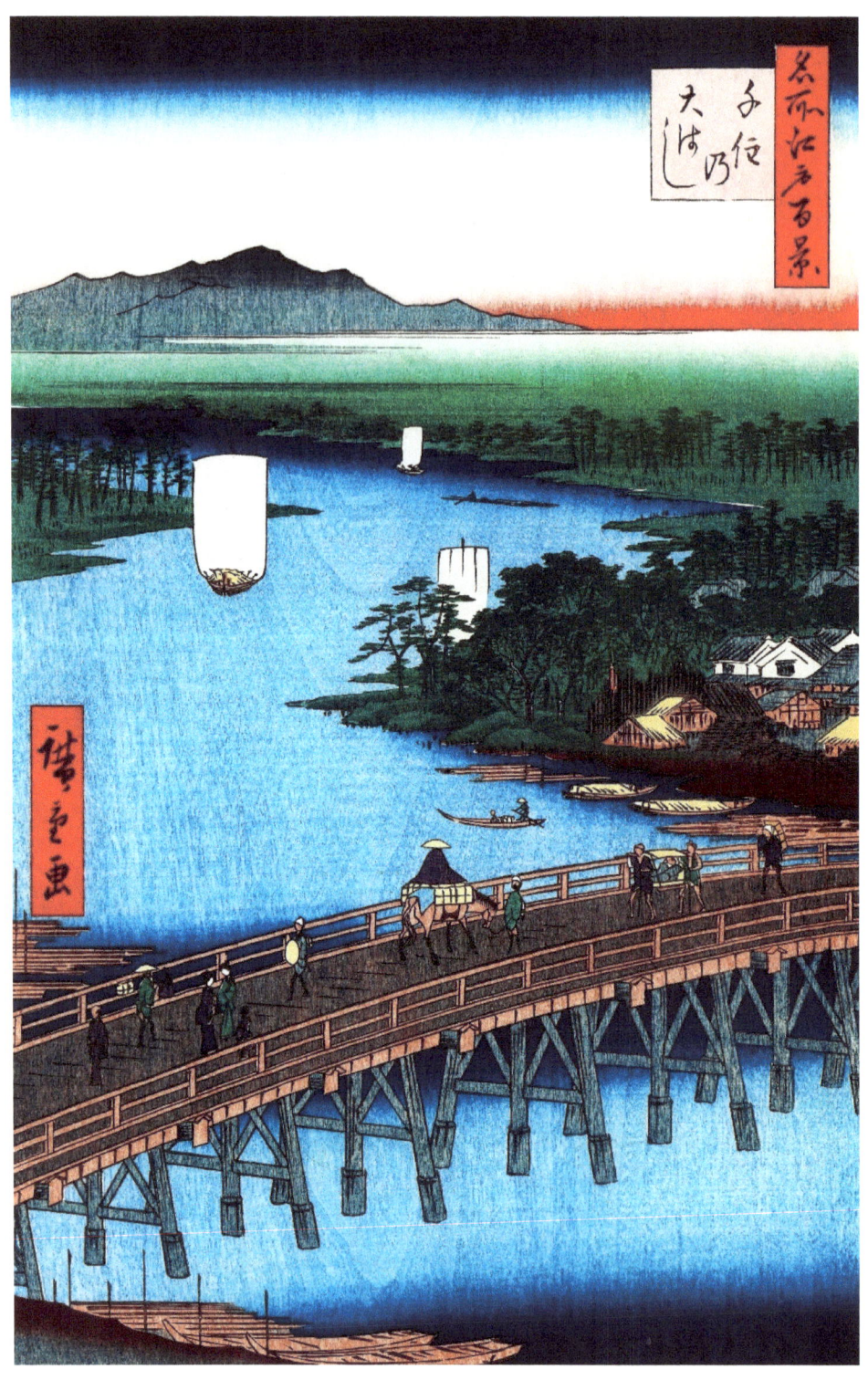

Senju no Ōhashi.

Pedestrians and man on horseback crossing the Senju bridge spanning the Sumida River, with a cluster of buildings on the right, sailboats on the river, and mountains in the background.

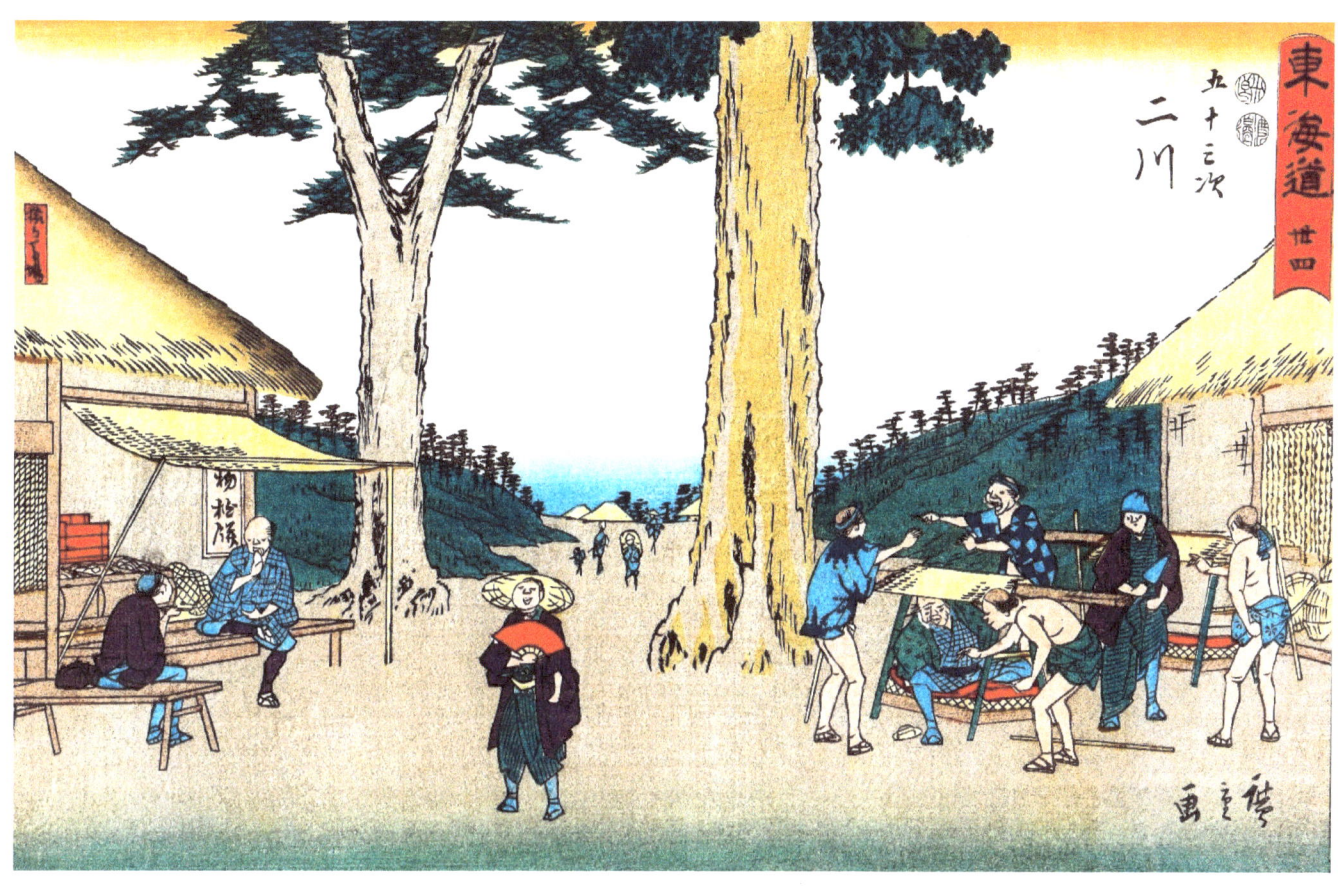

Futagawa.

Travelers with palanquins and approaching on foot, a shop with the merchant sitting on a bench in front, at the Futagawa station on the Tōkaidō Road.

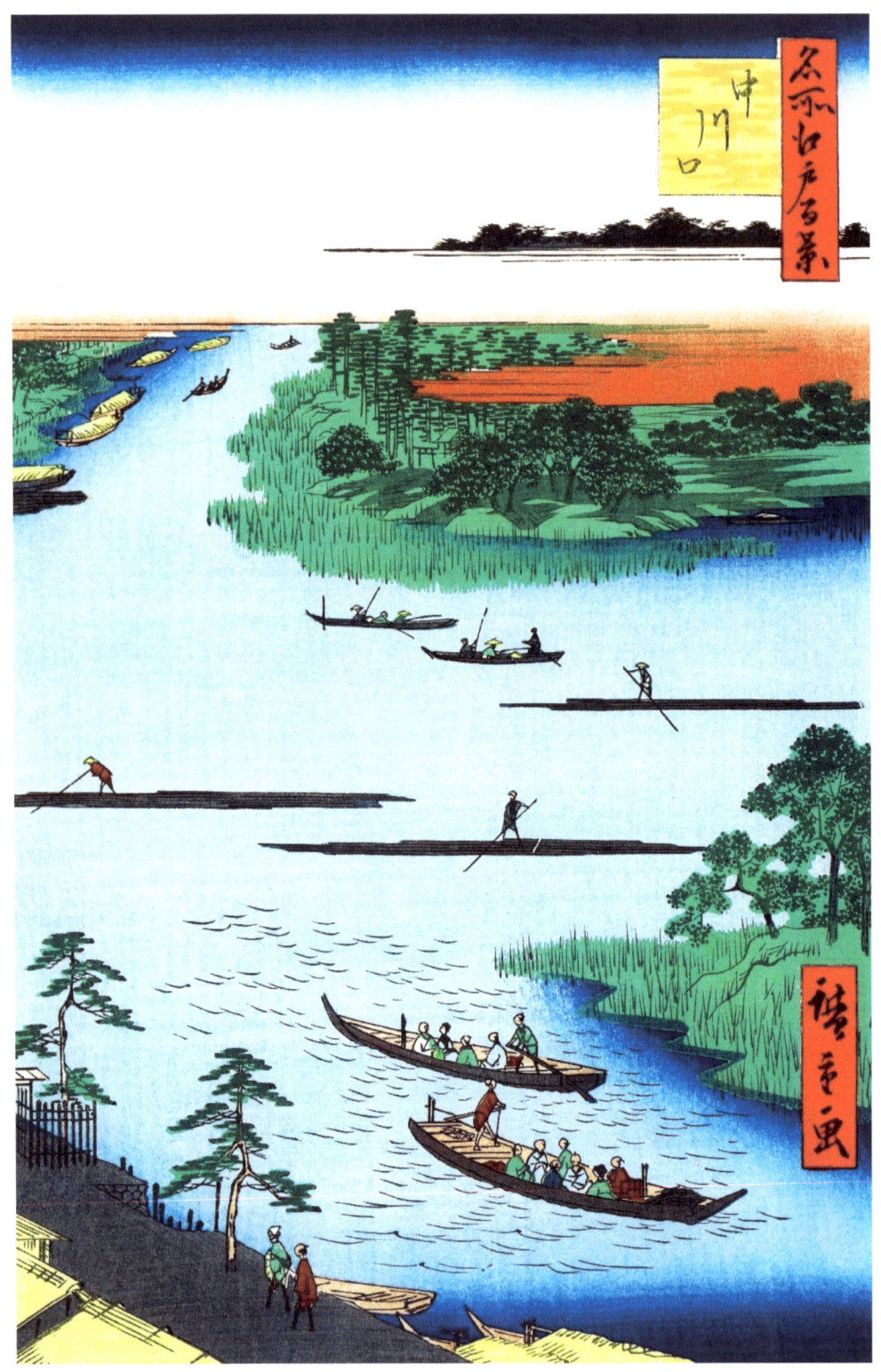

Nakagawaguchi.

The confluence of rivers at the mouth of the Naka River with ferry boats transporting passengers and boats or barges transporting lumber.

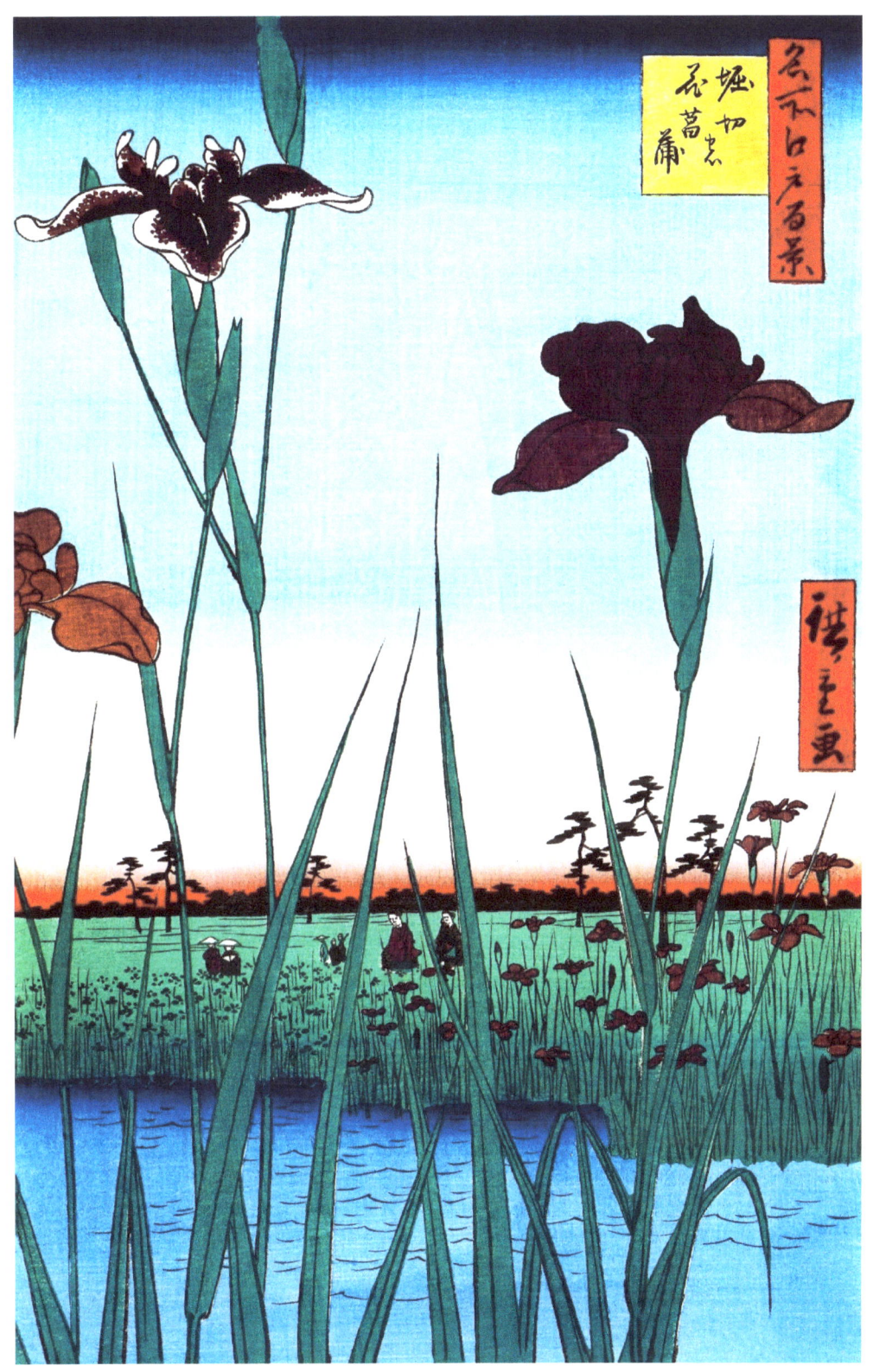

Horikiri no hanashōbu.

Irises growing in a large garden.

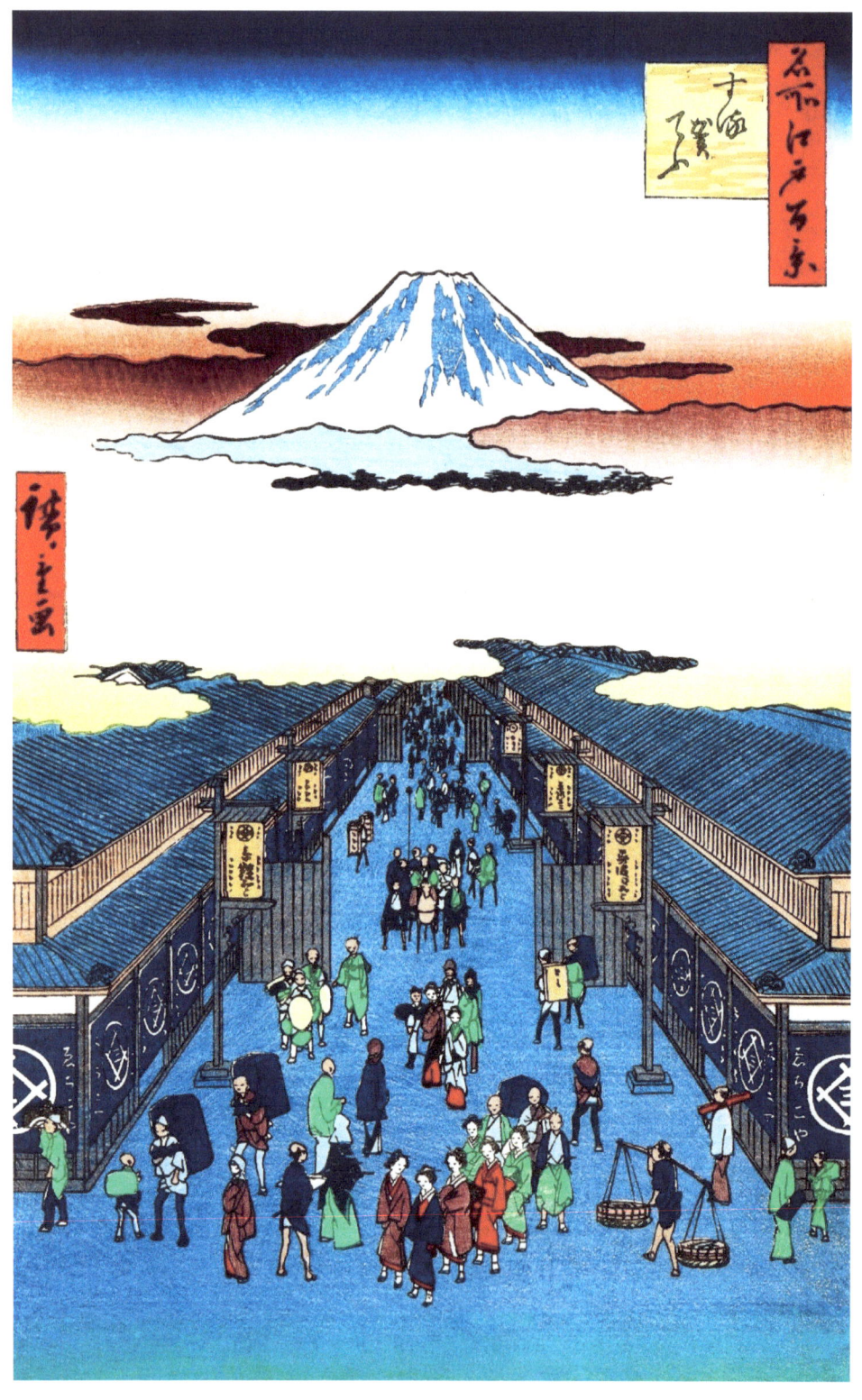

Suruga-chō.

Perspective view looking down commercial street with many pedestrians and porters, also shows Mount Fuji in the distance, above the clouds.

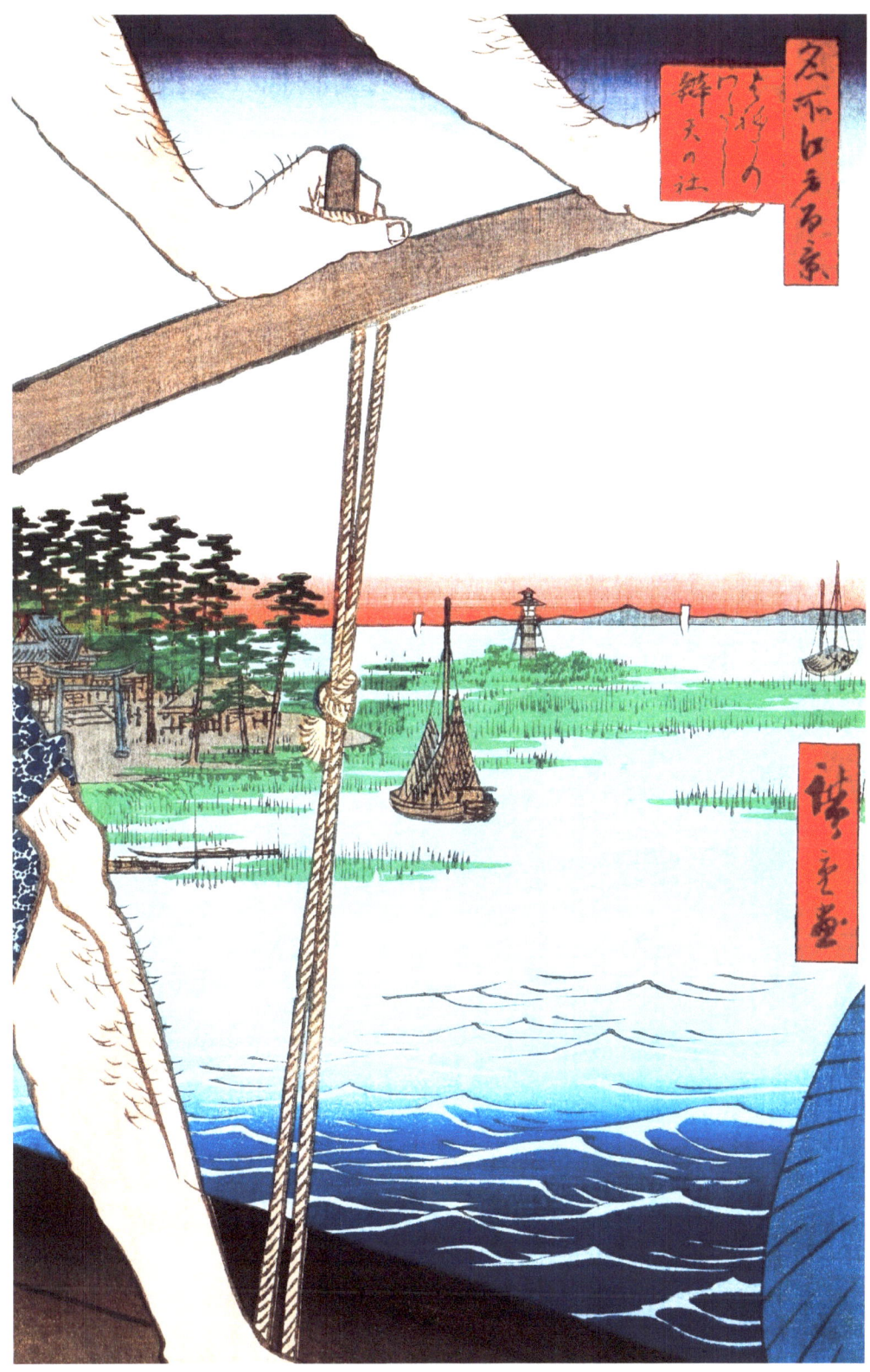

Haneda no watashi benten no yashiro.

A man at the helm on the Haneda ferry with the Benten Shrine in the distance.

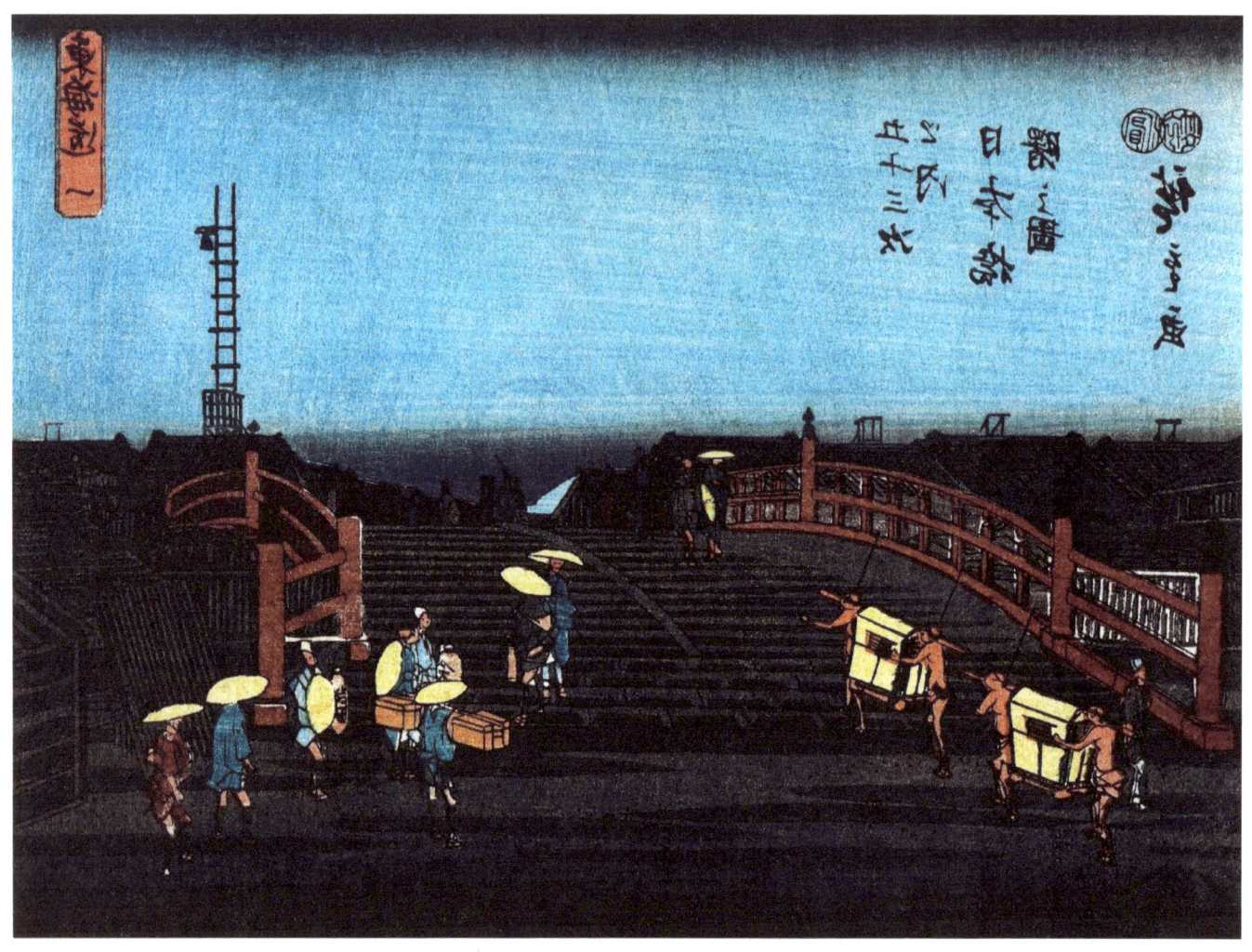

Nihonbashi akebono no zu.

Porters carrying sedan chairs and pedestrians crossing the Nihon Bridge at dawn.

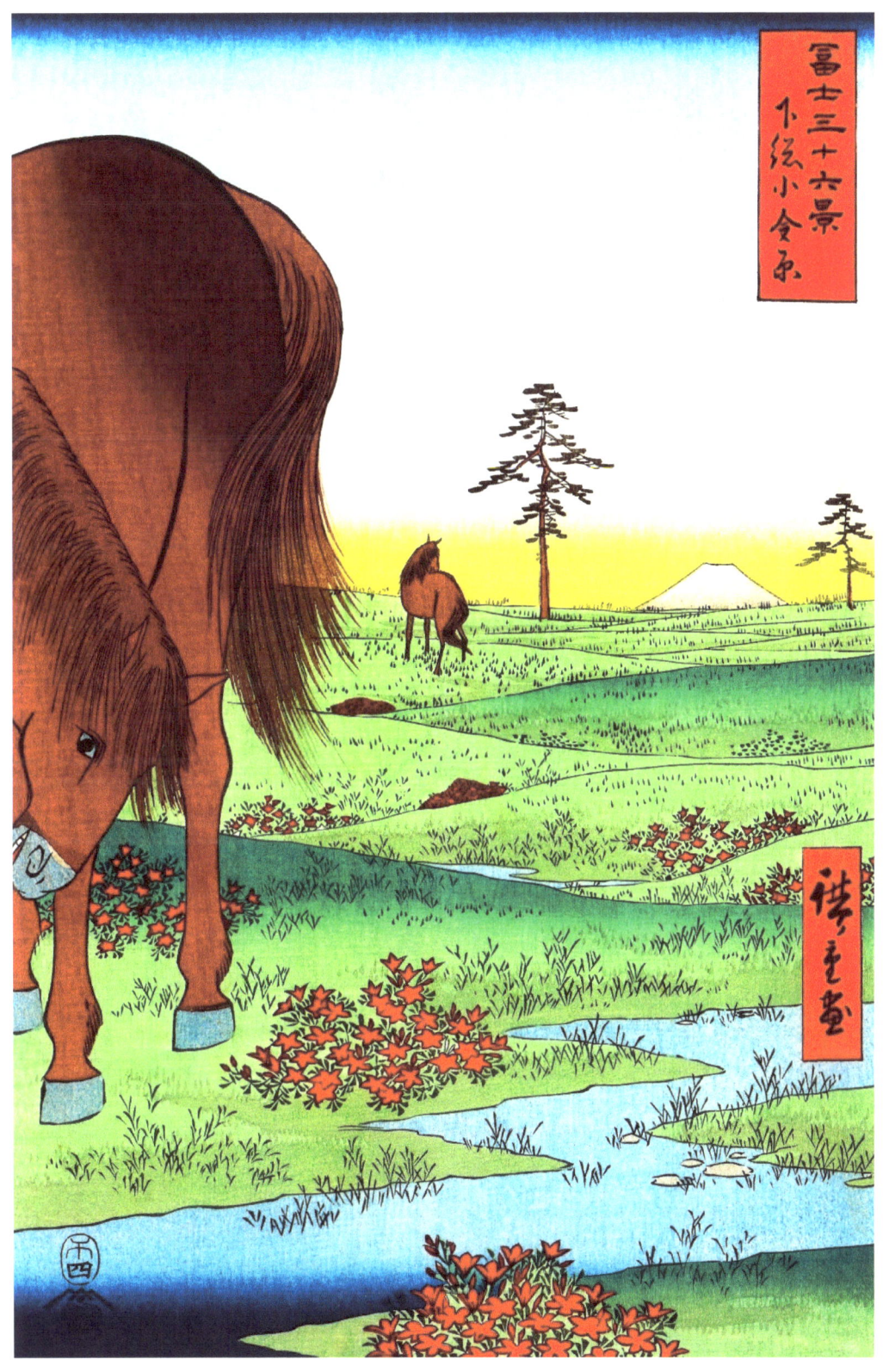

Shimōsa koganehara.

Two horses grazing on open plains with a view of Mount Fuji in the background.

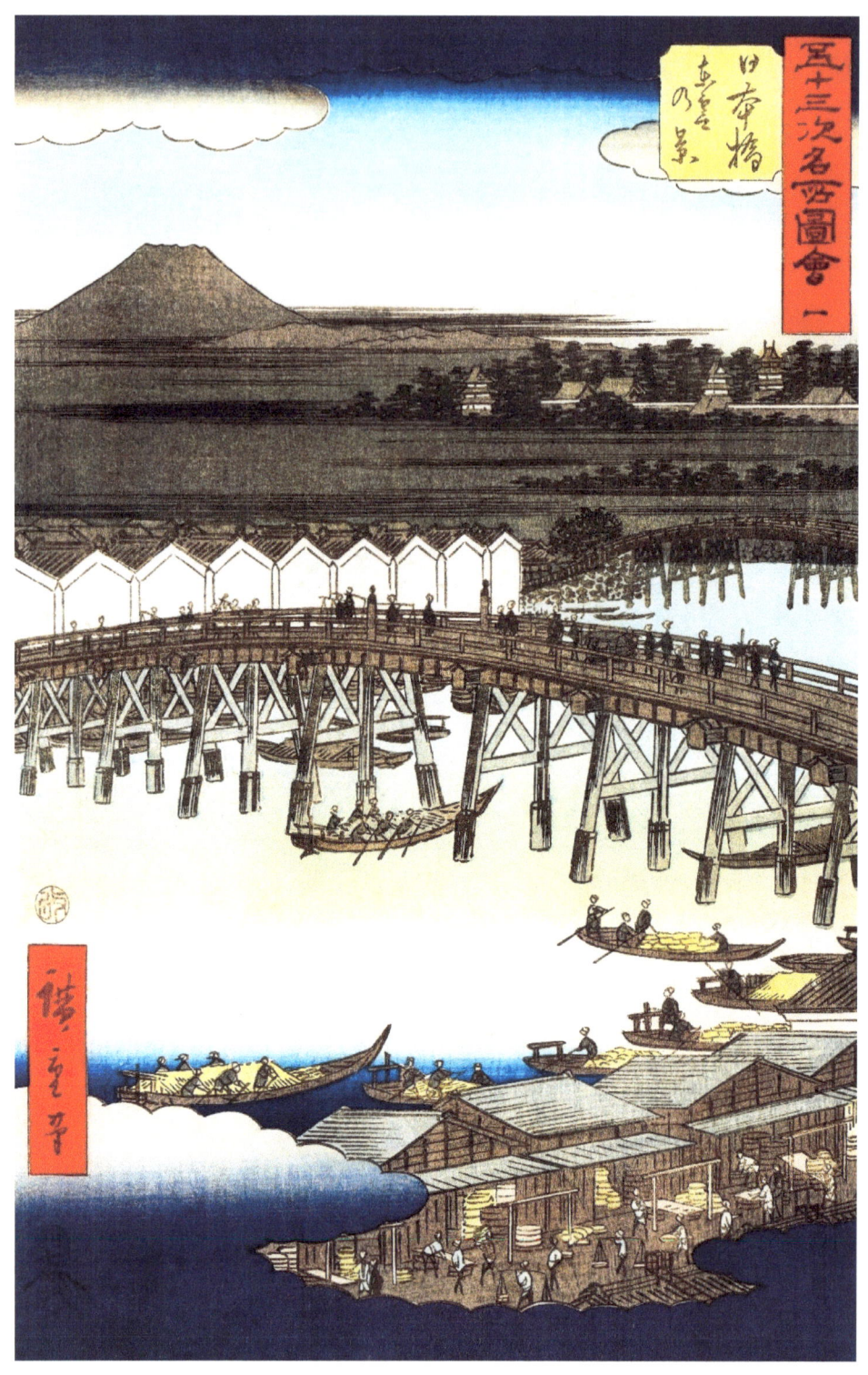

Nihonbashi.

A bird's-eye view of the Japan Bridge with boats on the river, shops in the foreground, large buildings across the river, another bridge and a temple in the near distance, and Mount Fuji in the background, at the Nihonbashi station on the Tōkaidō Road.

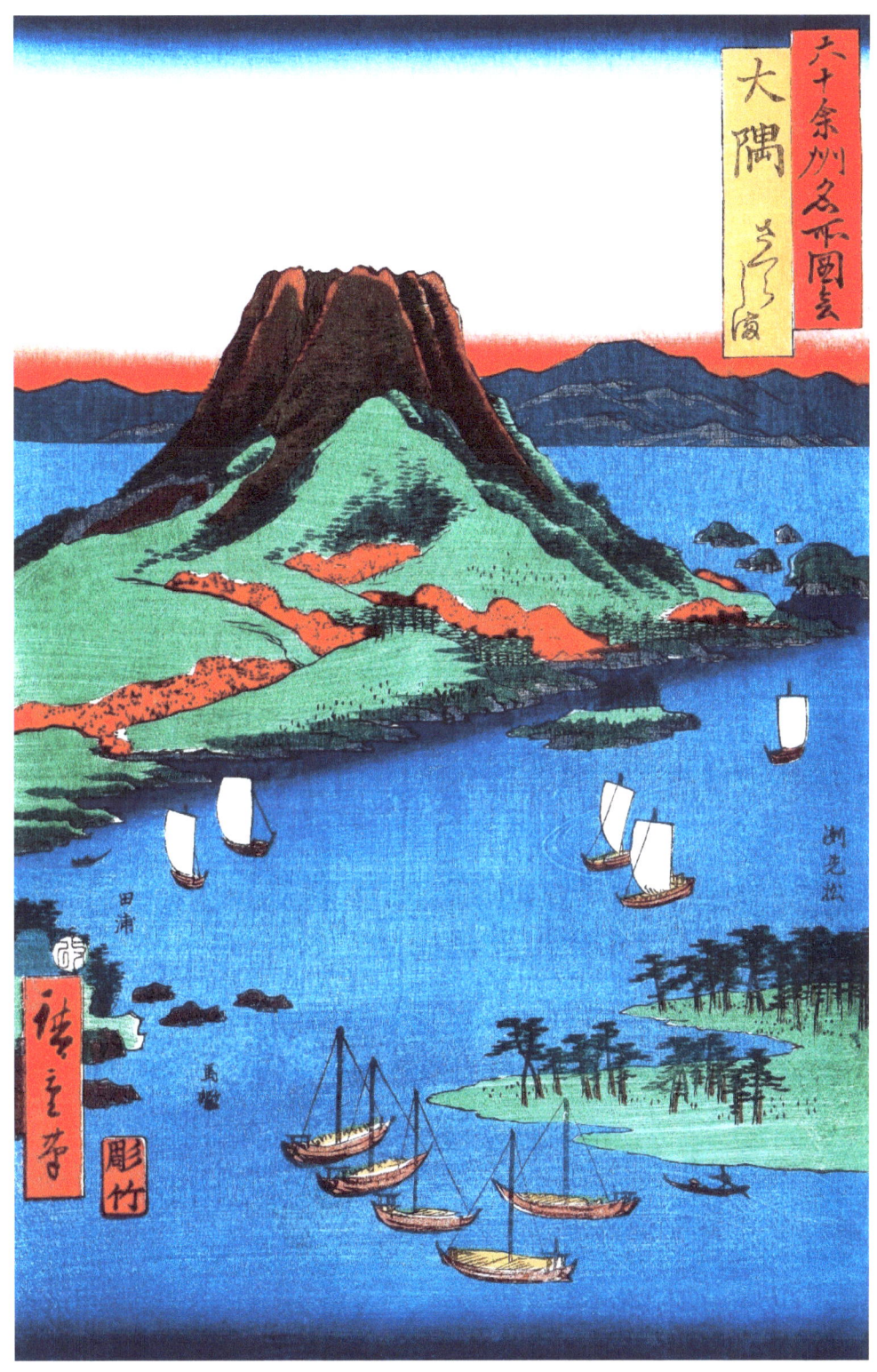

Ōsumi.

The volcano Sakurajima at Ōsumi on Sakura Island, with sailing ships in the sea around the island.

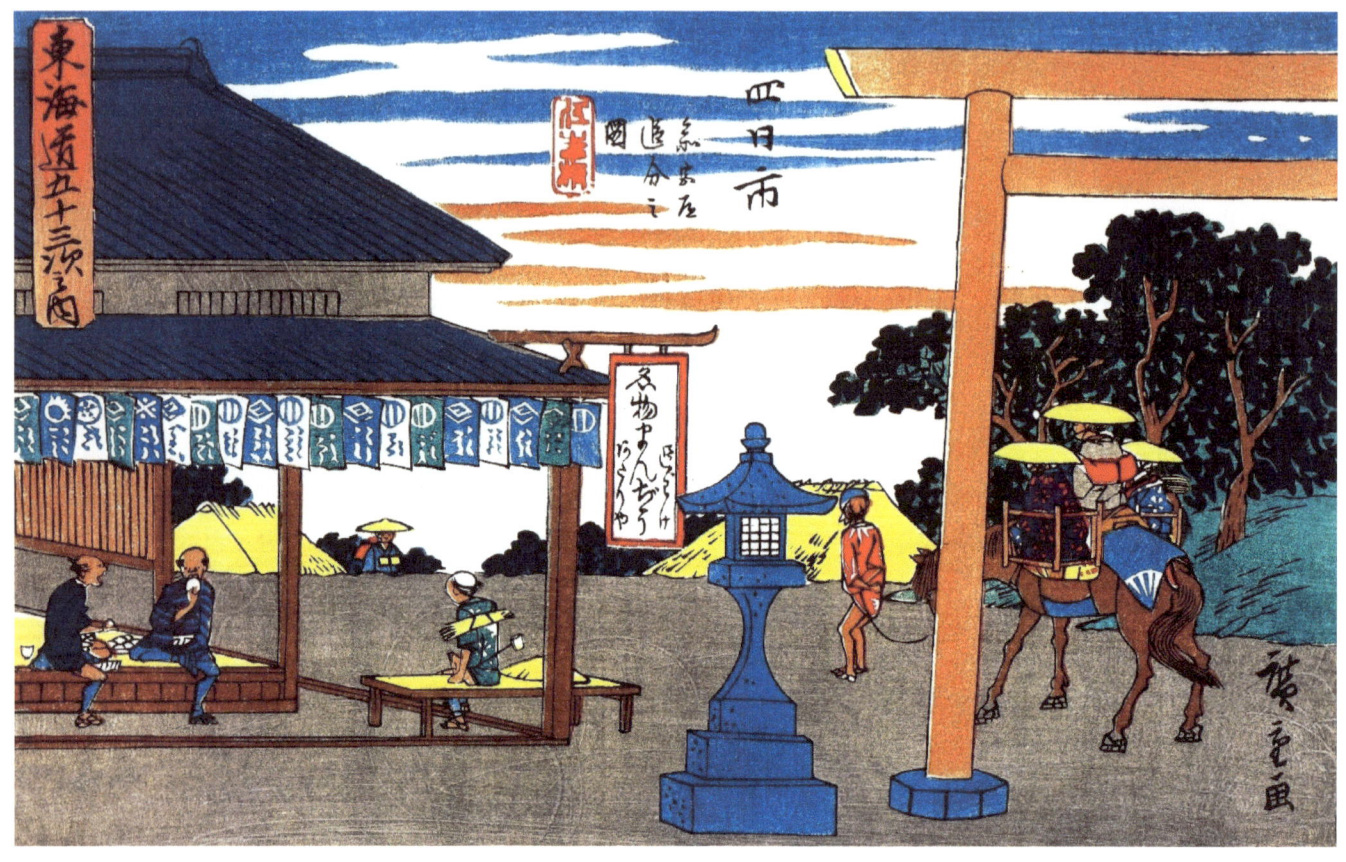

Yokkaichi.

Travelers at, and passing on horseback, a rest stop near a small shrine and a torii at the Yokkaichi station on the Tōkaidō Road.

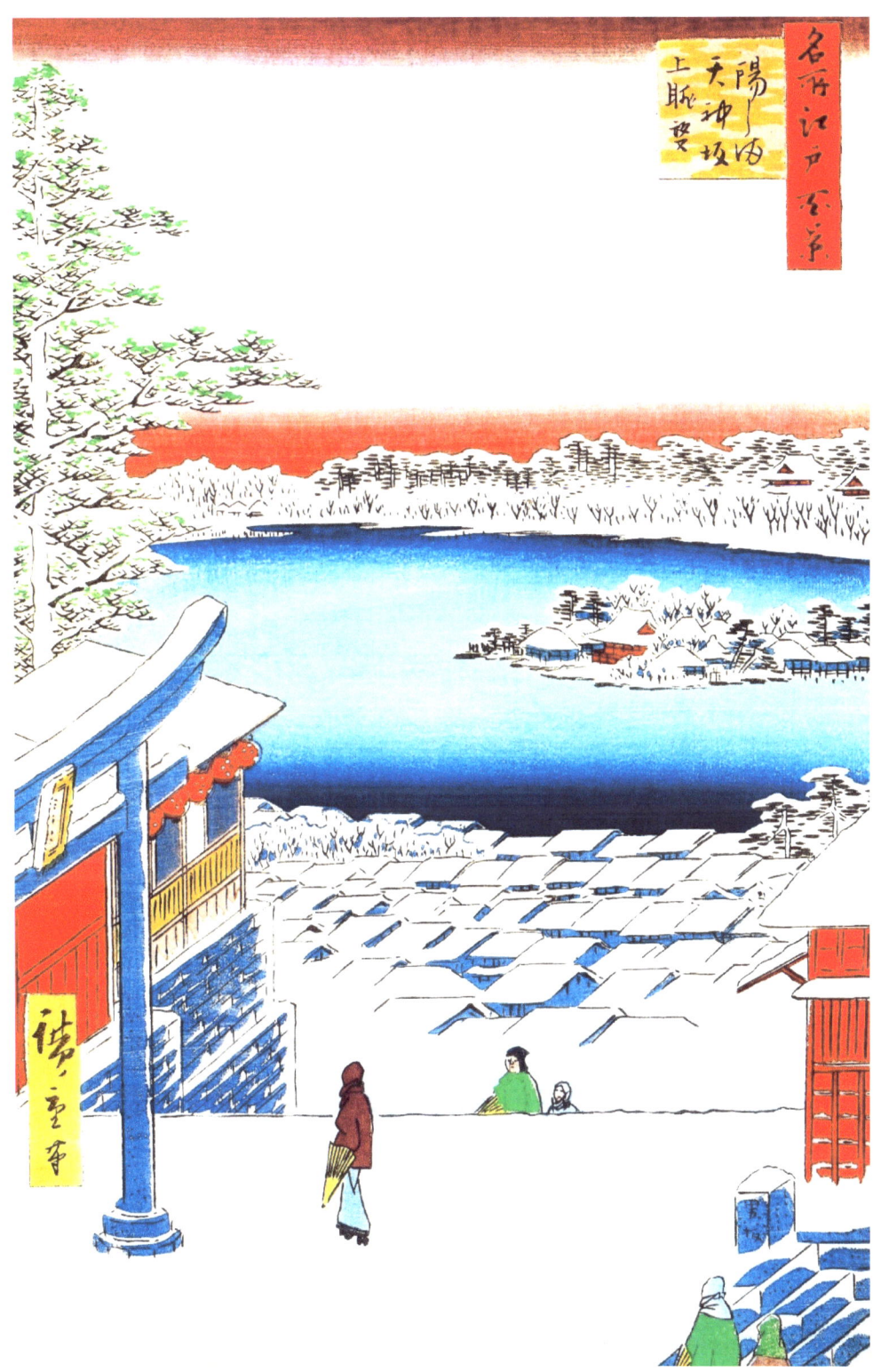

Yushima tenjin sakaue chōbō.

Pedestrians walking in the snow at the Yushima Tenjin shrine, with torii on the left, on a hilltop above the city.

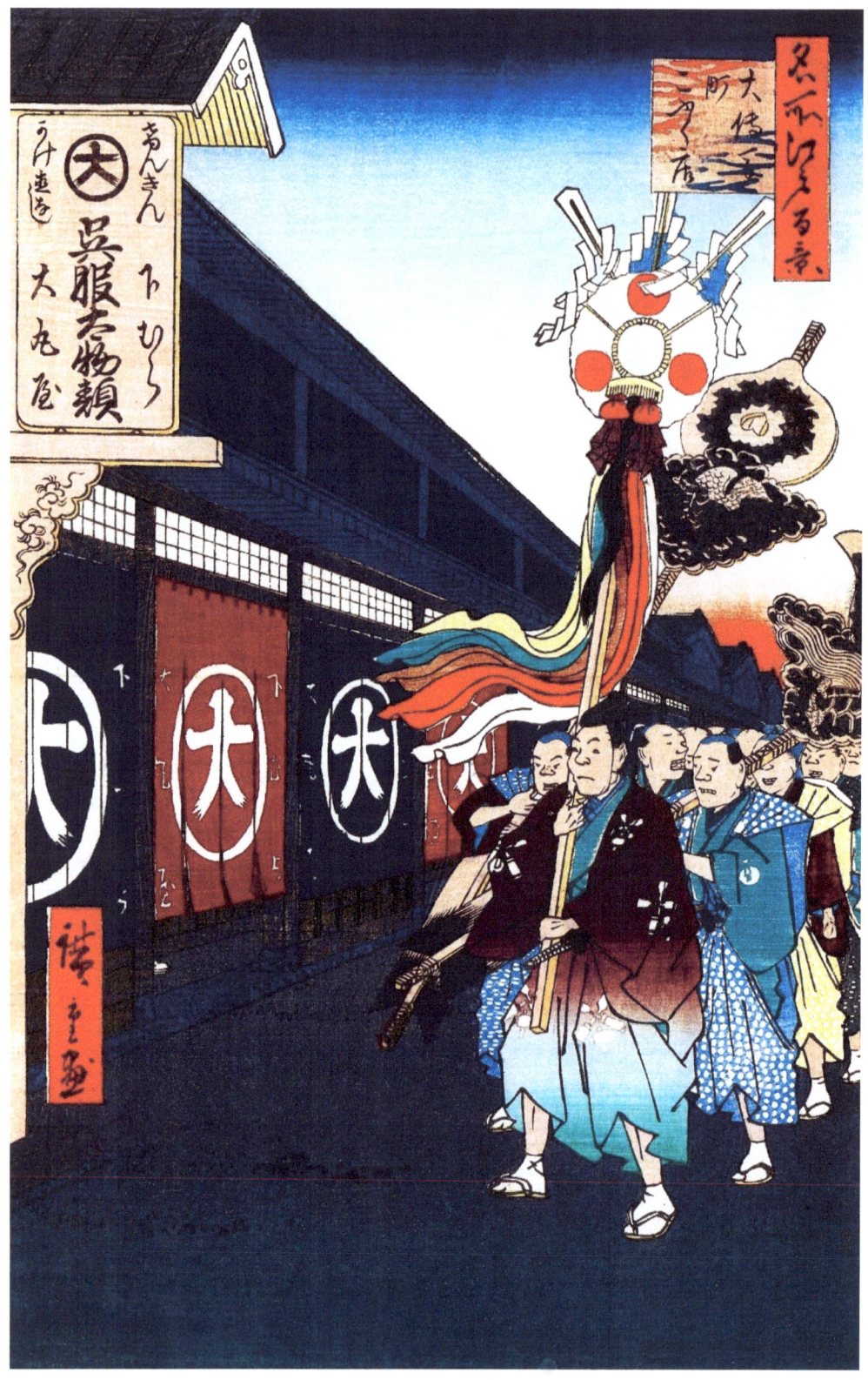

Ōdenmachō gofukudana.

Several men with decorations and banners on long poles marching past a clothing shop.

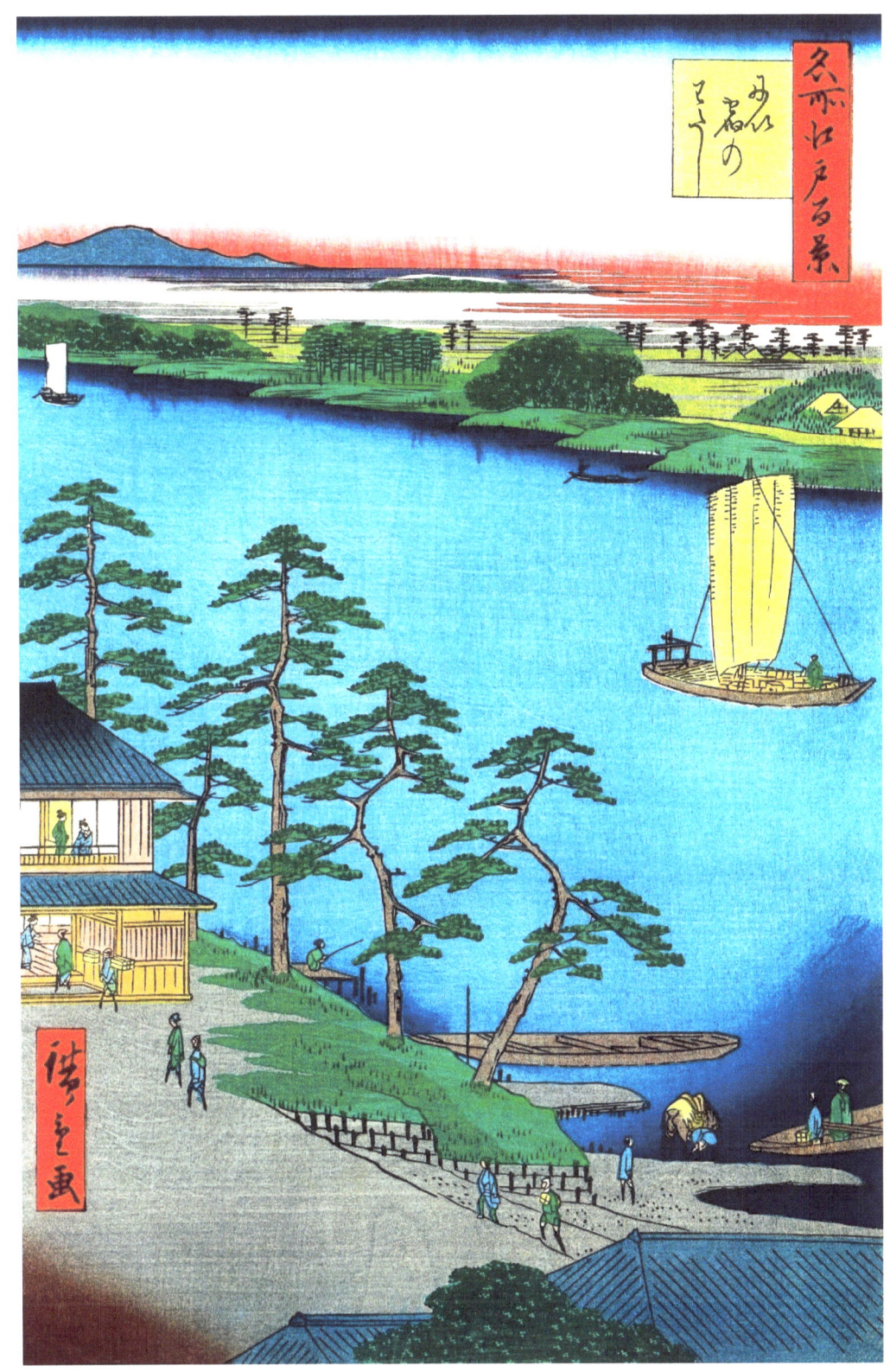

Niijuku no watashi.

The terminal at the Niijuku ferry, with large building on the left and sailboat on the river.

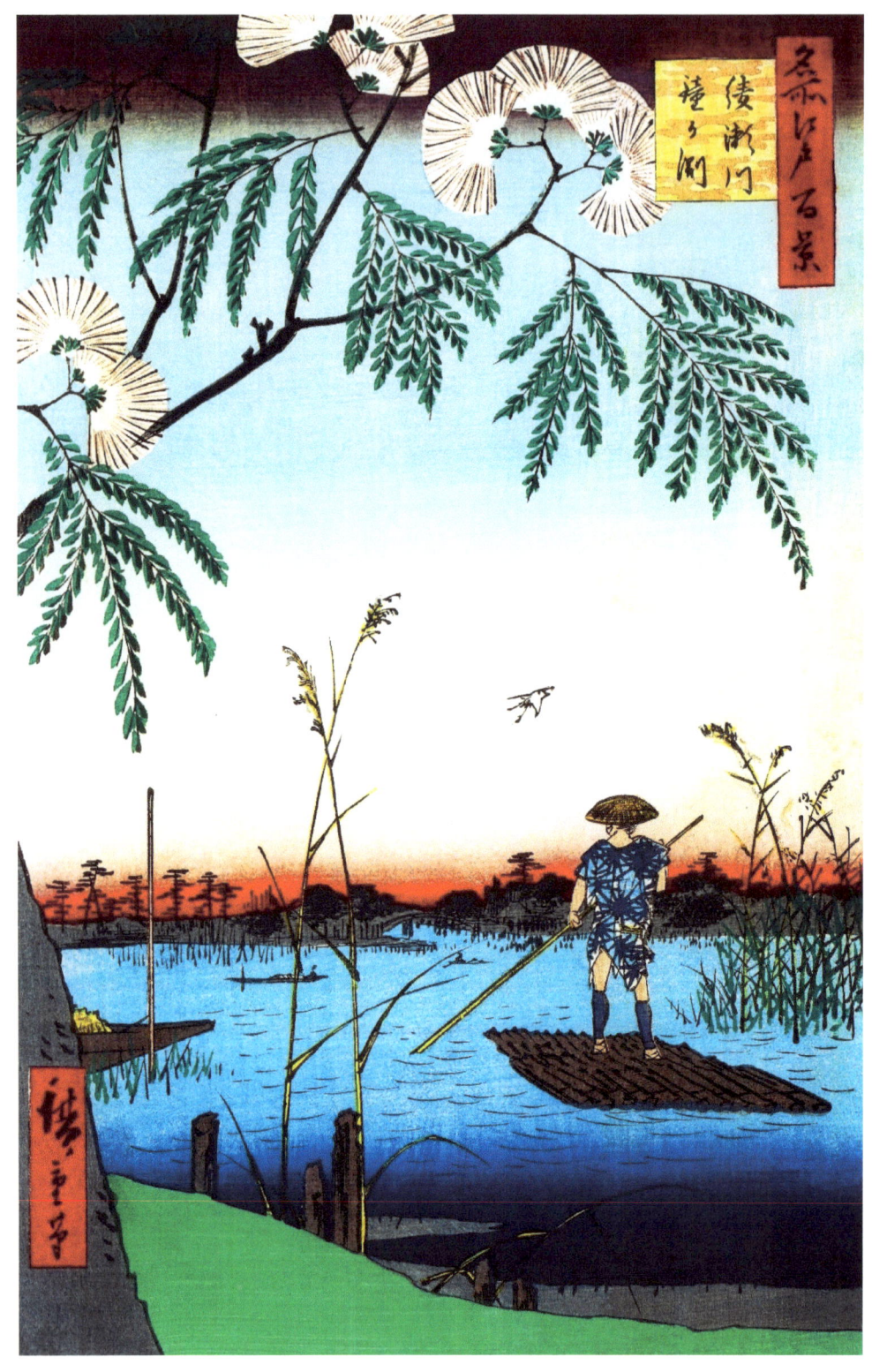

Ayasegawa kanegafuchi.

A man poling a raft among reeds in marsh area of river with blossoming mimosa tree in the foreground.

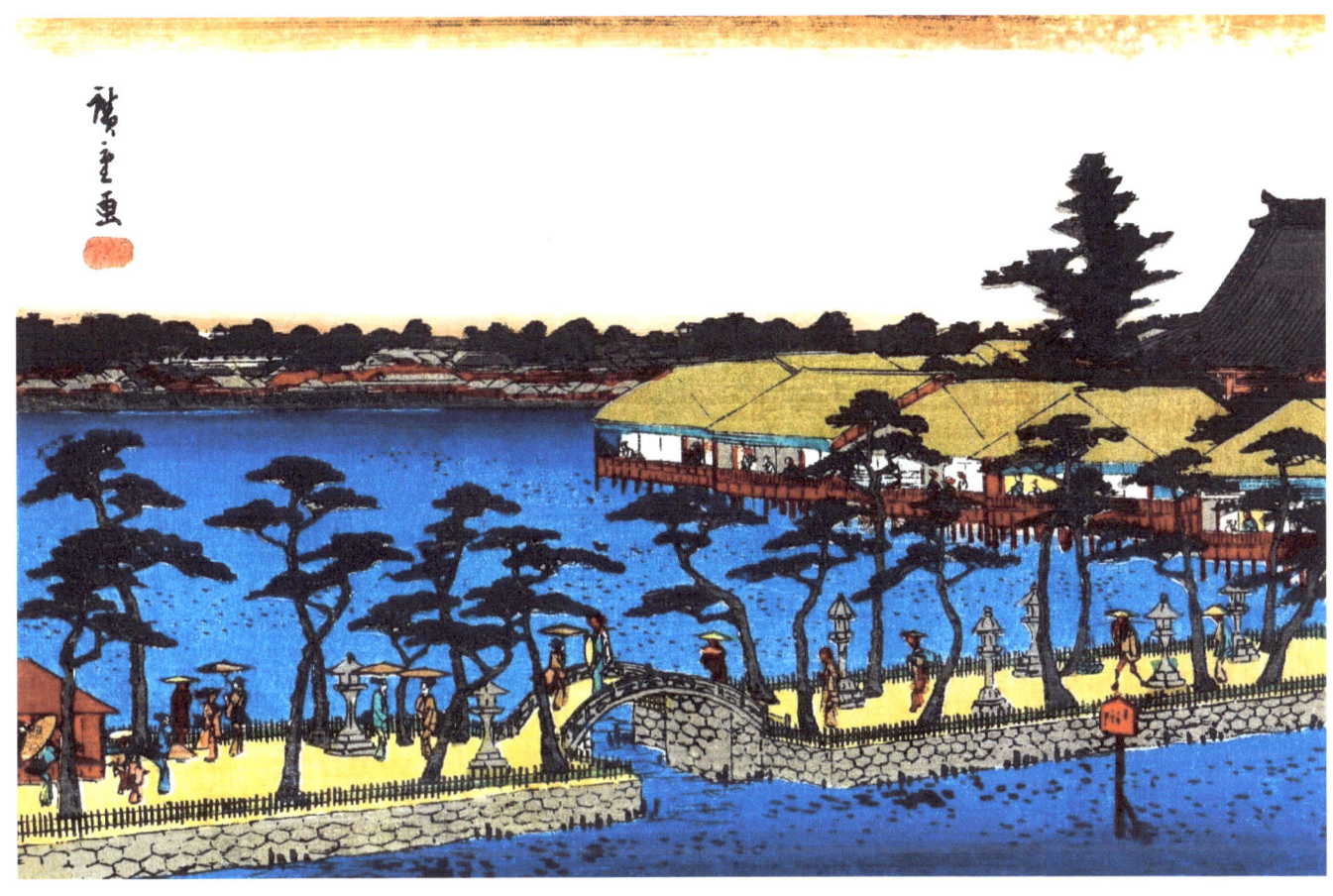

Shinobazu no ike benten no hokora.

Pedestrians on a bridge across Shinobazu Pond leading to the Benten shrine; pine trees along the bridge, buildings on pilings extending into the pond, and buildings of the town in the background.

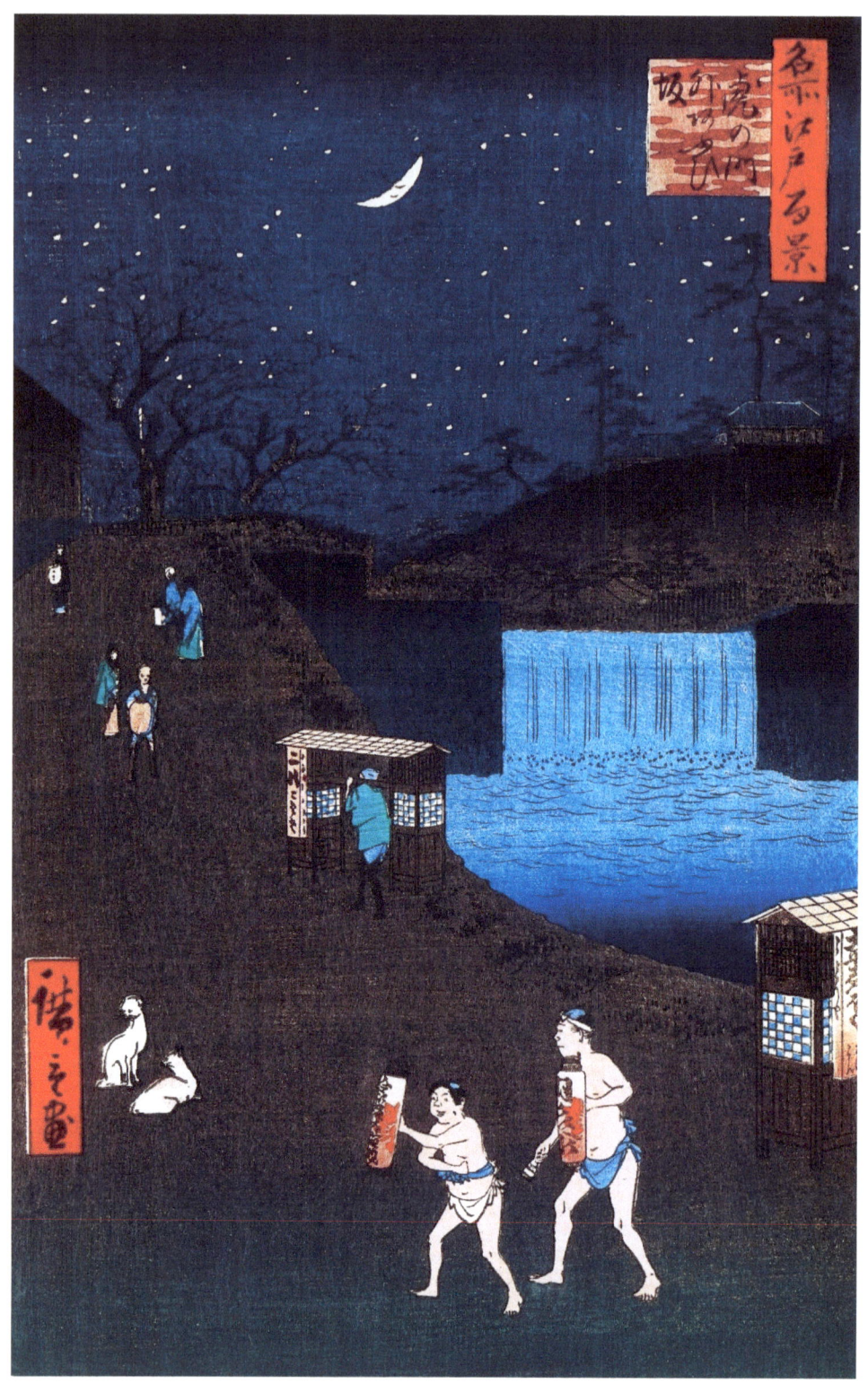

Toranomon-soto aoizaka.

Pedestrians, a porter or noodle vendor, and two men carrying lanterns on a walkway near waterfalls and the Aoi slope, beneath a crescent moon.

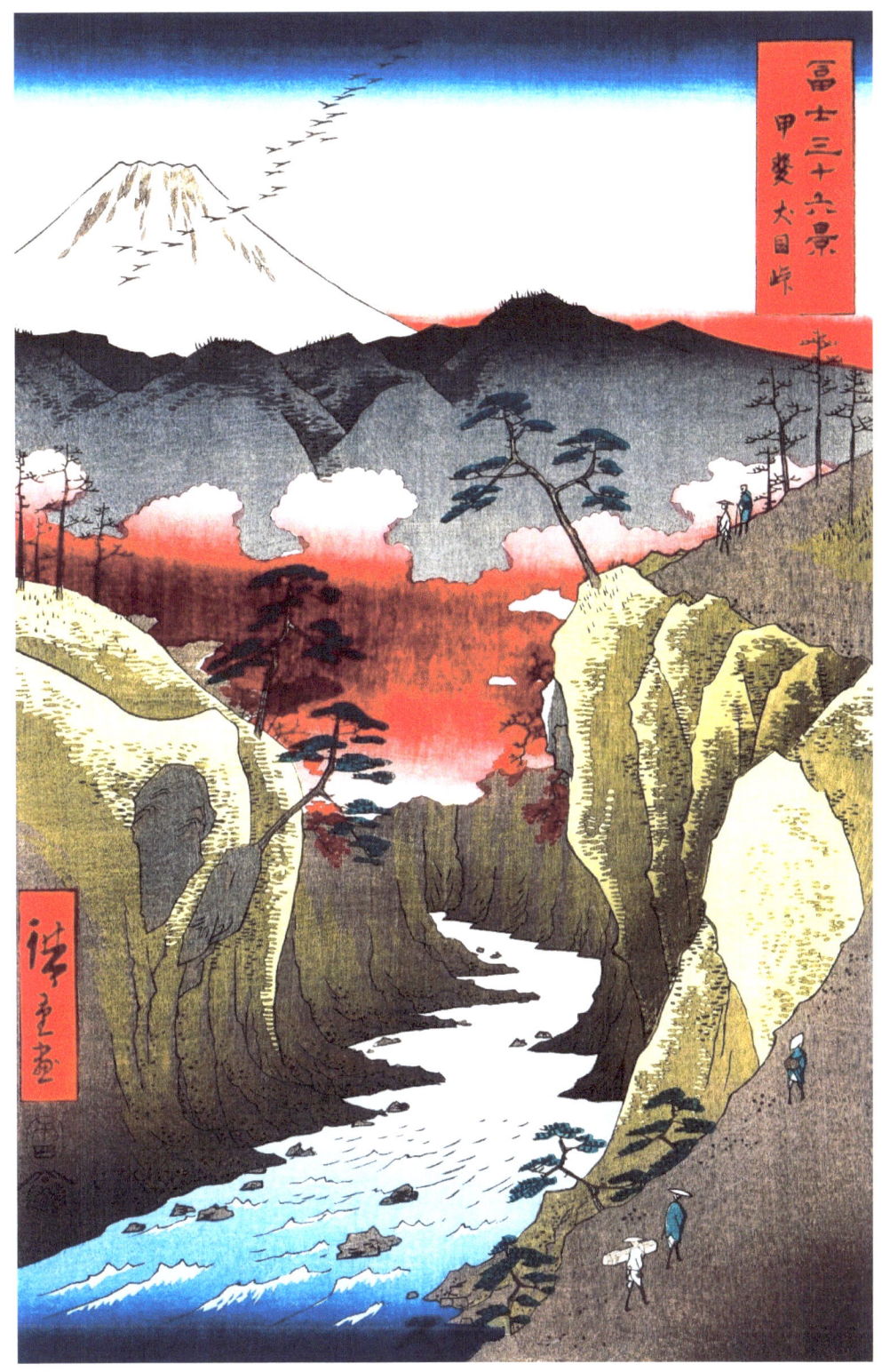

Kai inume tōge.

Travelers on a mountain pass along a steep canyon and river, with mountains and a view of Mount Fuji in the background.

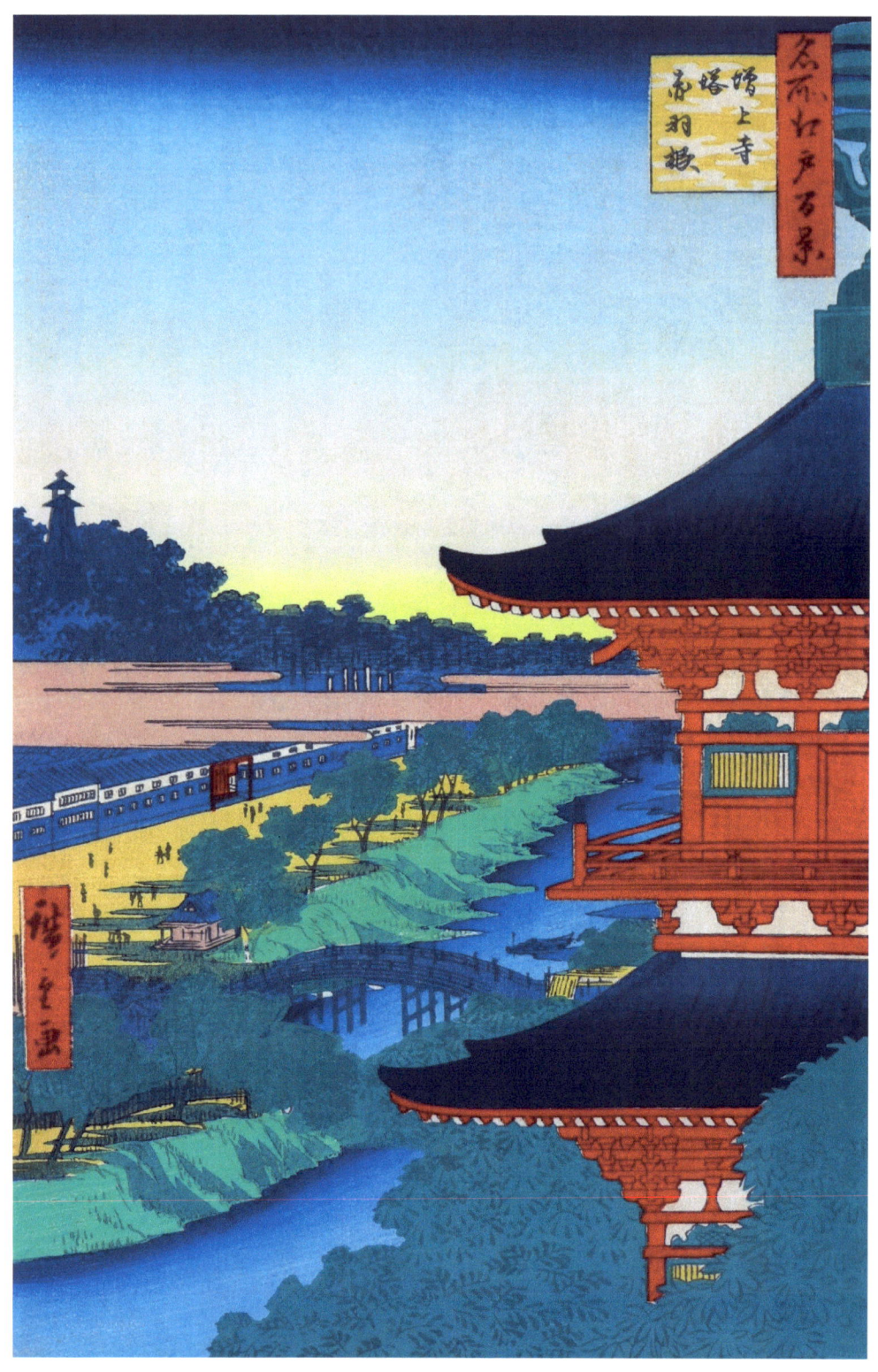

Zōjōji tō akabane.

A bird's-eye view from near the top of a pagoda with river, bridge, and temple in the distance.

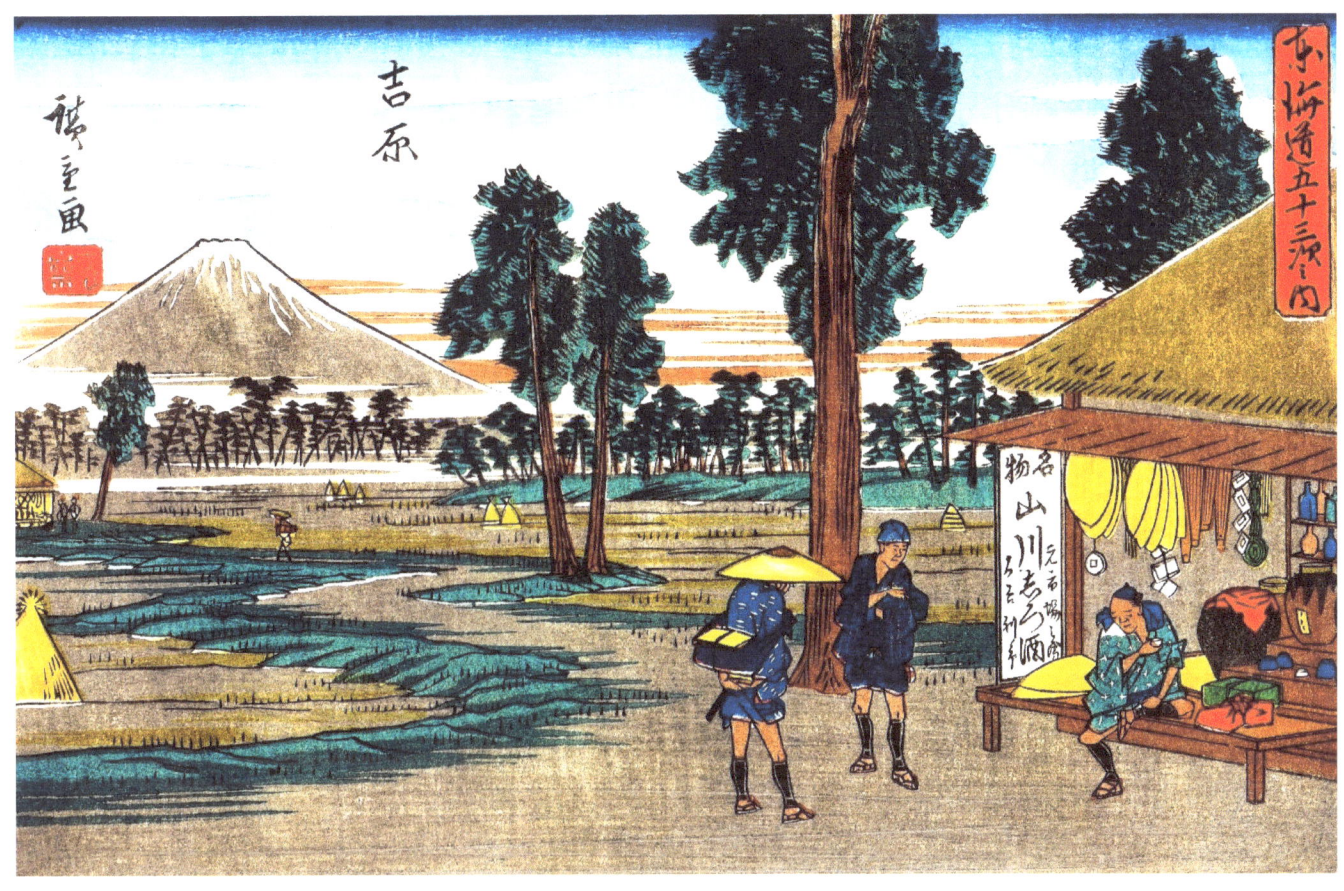

Yoshiwara.

Two travelers outside a shop, the vendor sitting on a table in front, also pine trees, haystacks, and a view of Mount Fuji in the background, at the Yoshiwara station on the Tōkaidō Road.

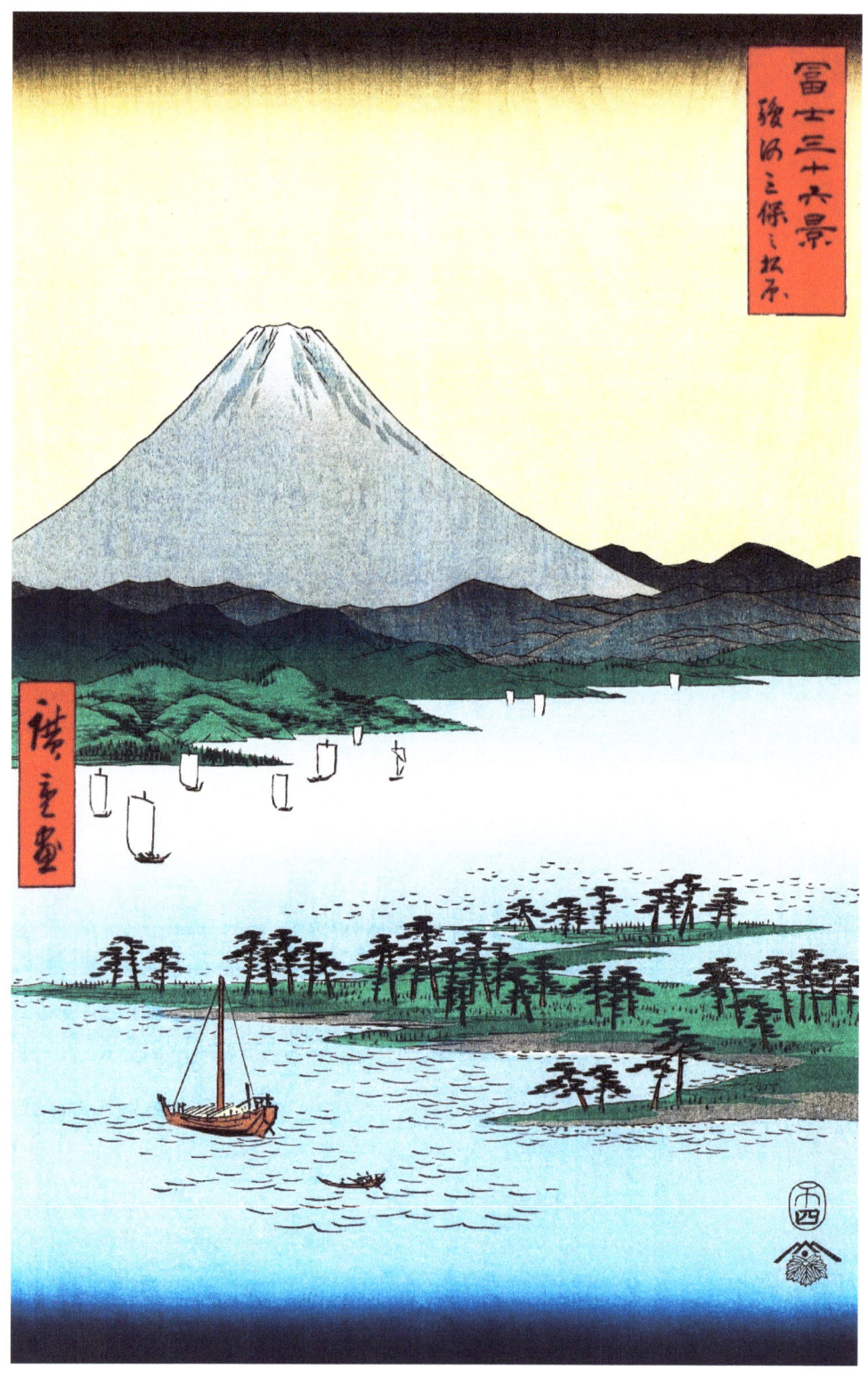

Suruga miho no matsubara.

A view of Mount Fuji with a pine grove on a promontory in the Suruga Bay surrounded by sailboats.

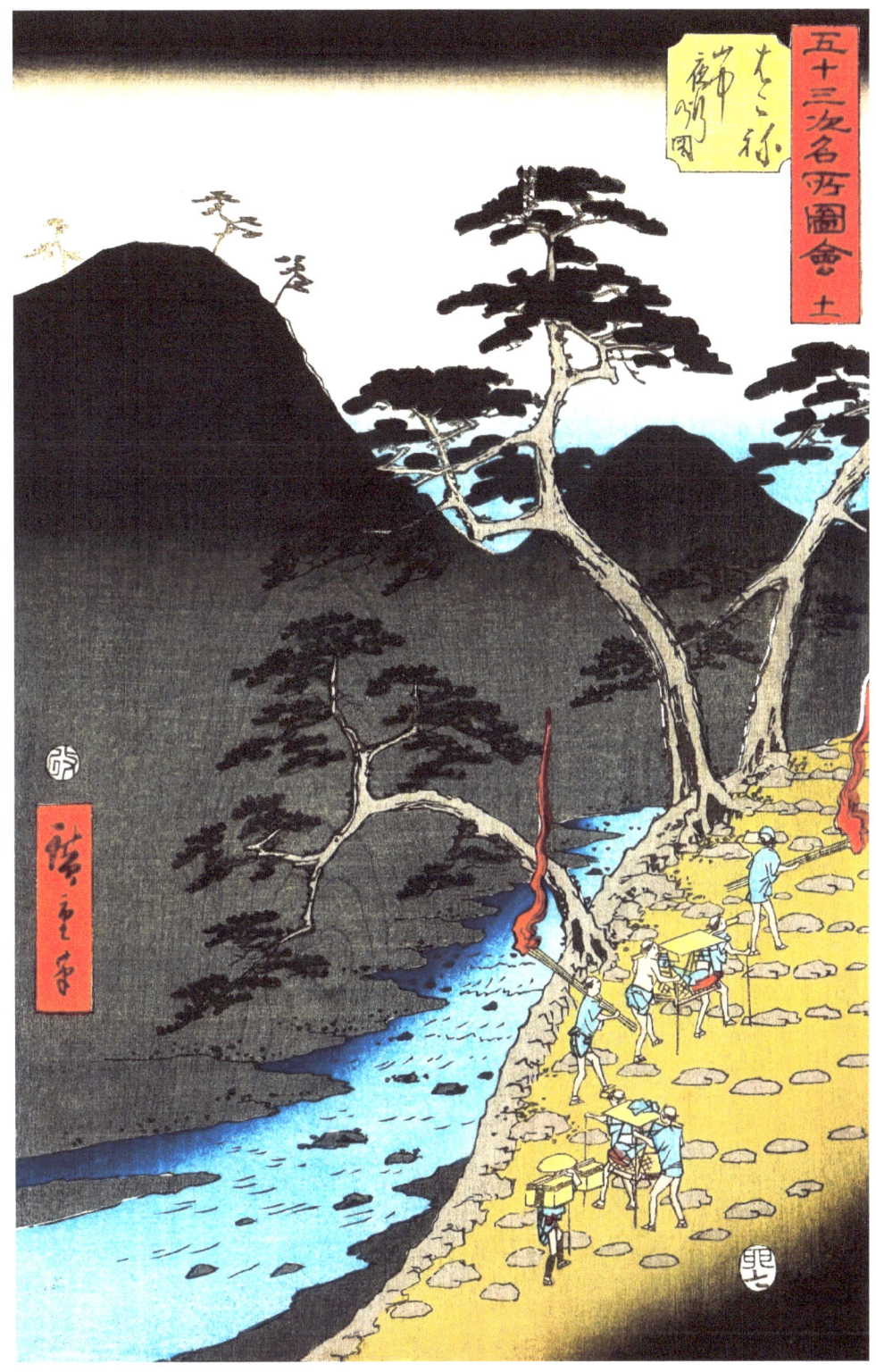

Hakone.

Travelers and porters crossing a steep pass in the mountains at the Hakone station on the Tōkaidō Road.

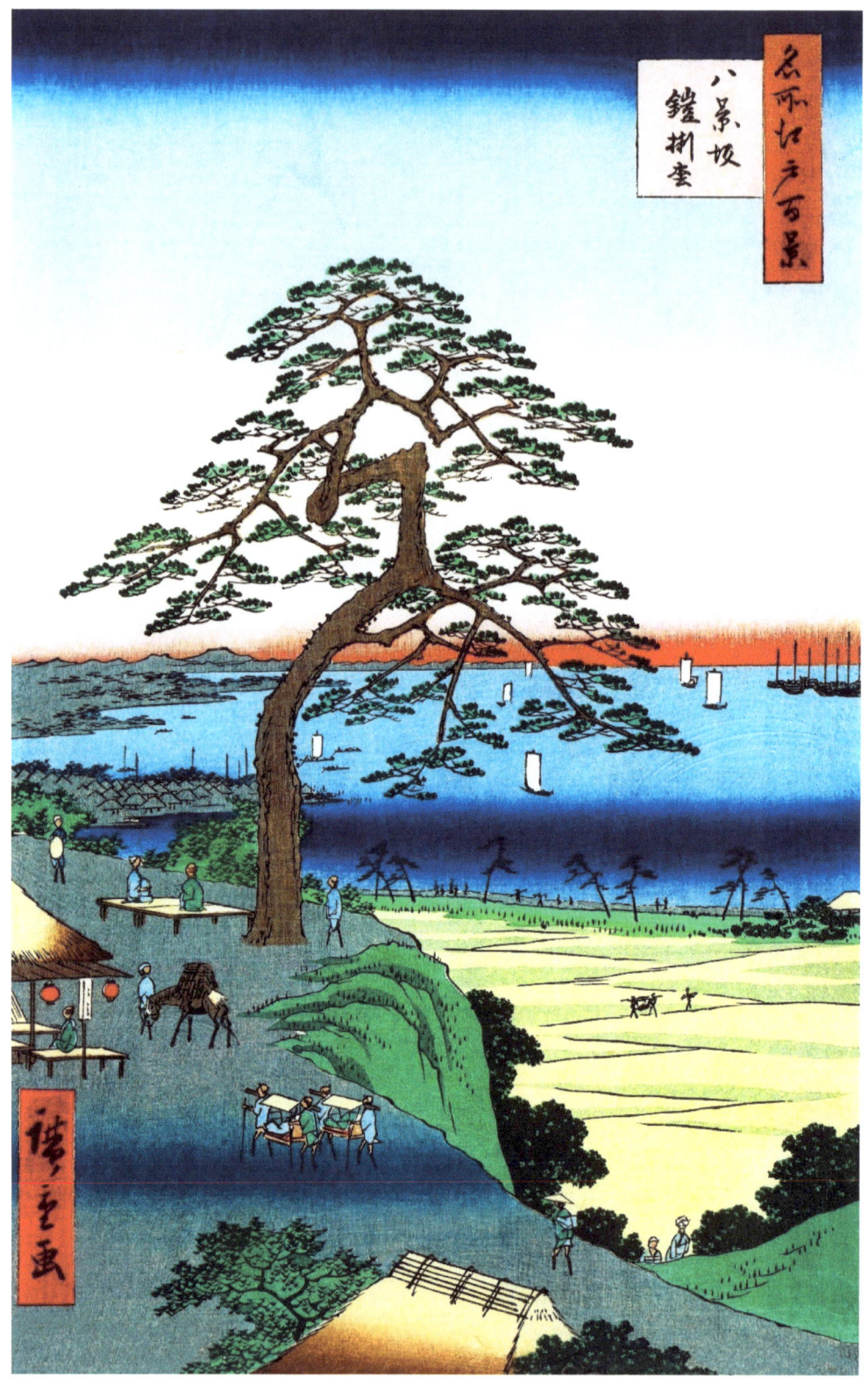

Hakkeisaka yoroikakematsu.

Travelers at rest stop on bluff with large pine tree near the harbor at Edo.

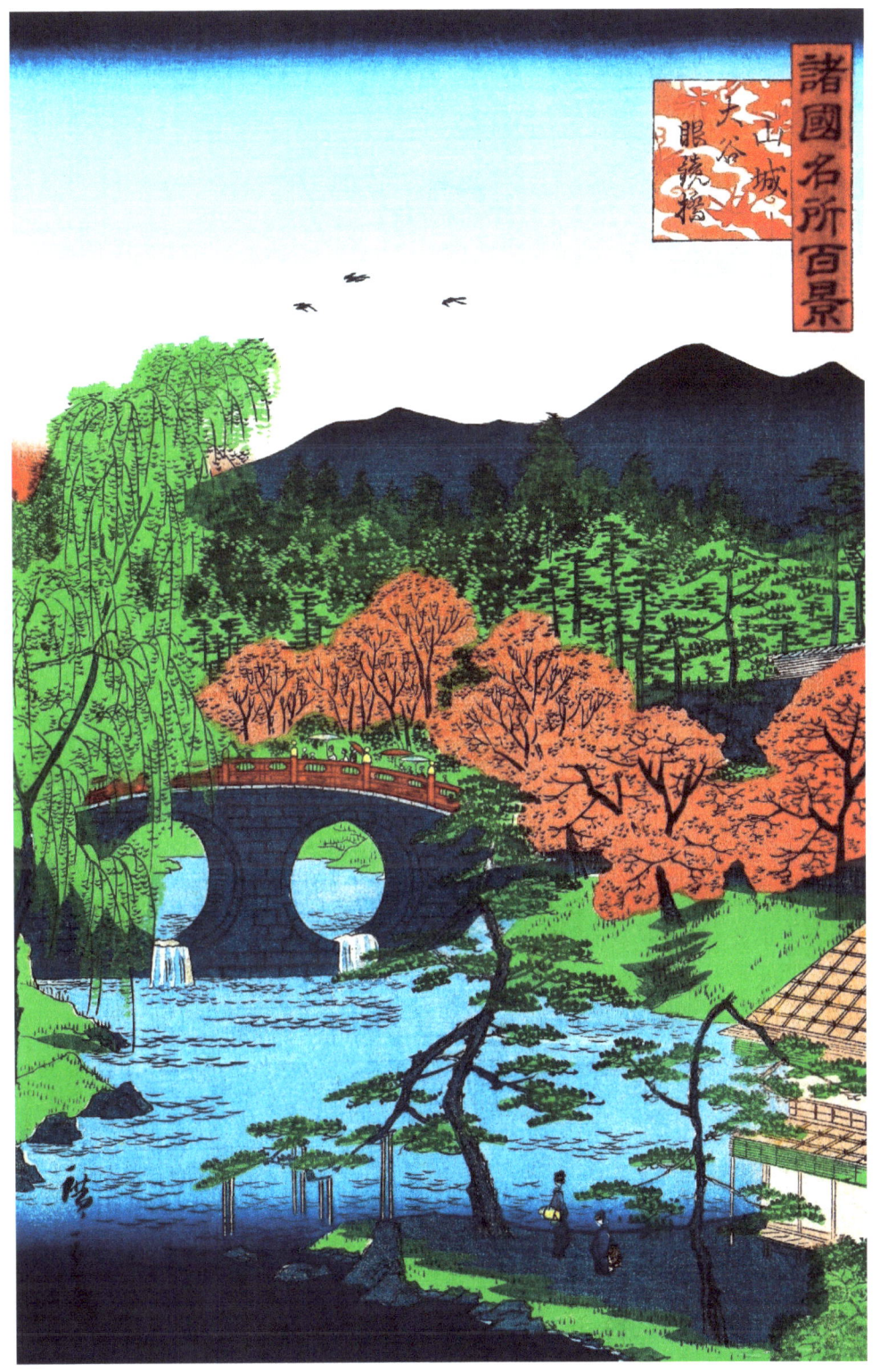

Yamashiro ōtani meganebashi.

The Megane Bridge spanning a river at Ōtani Temple, with blossoming trees, in the Yamashiro Province.

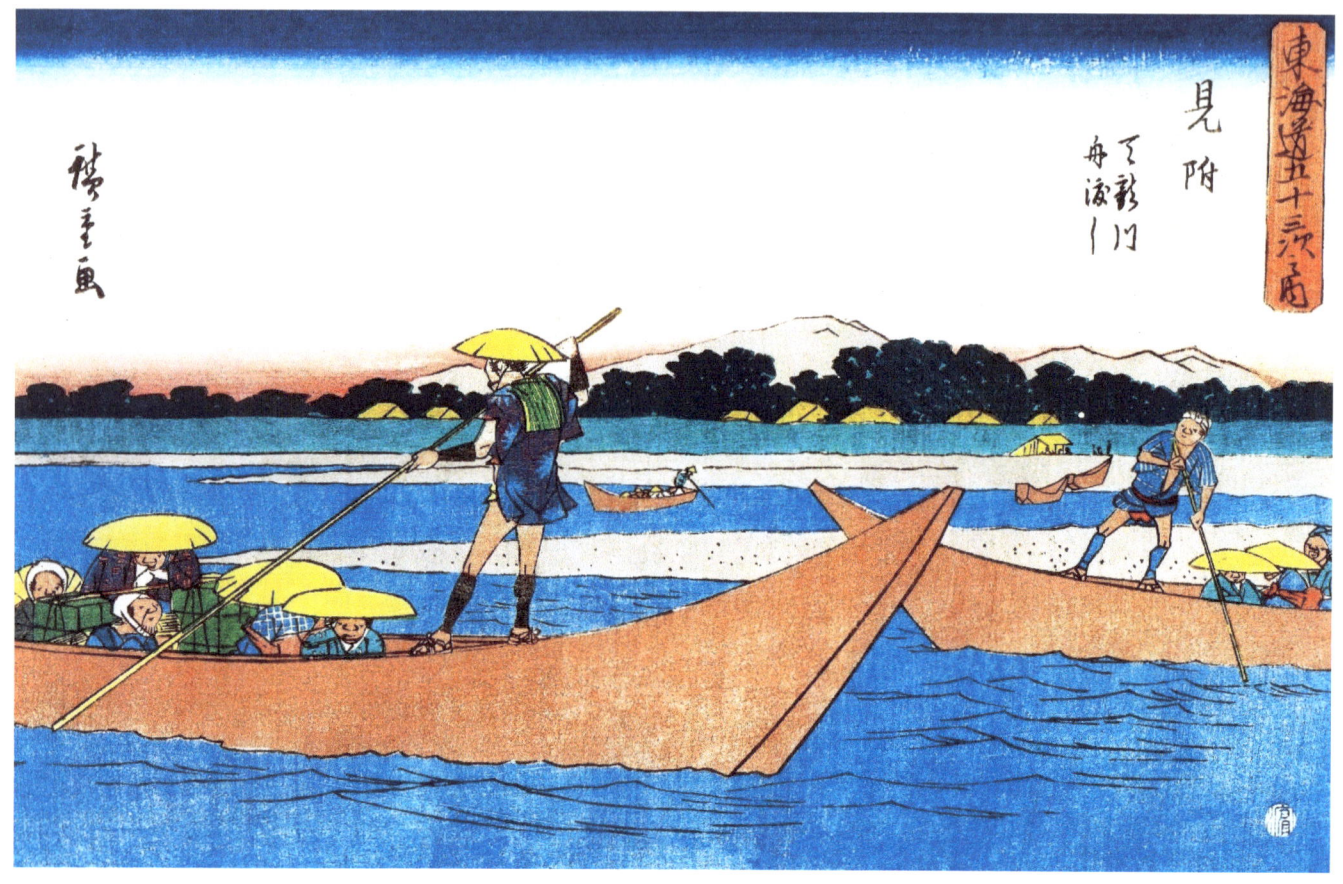

Mitsuke.

Men poling boats filled with travelers near the Mitsuke station on the Tōkaidō Road.

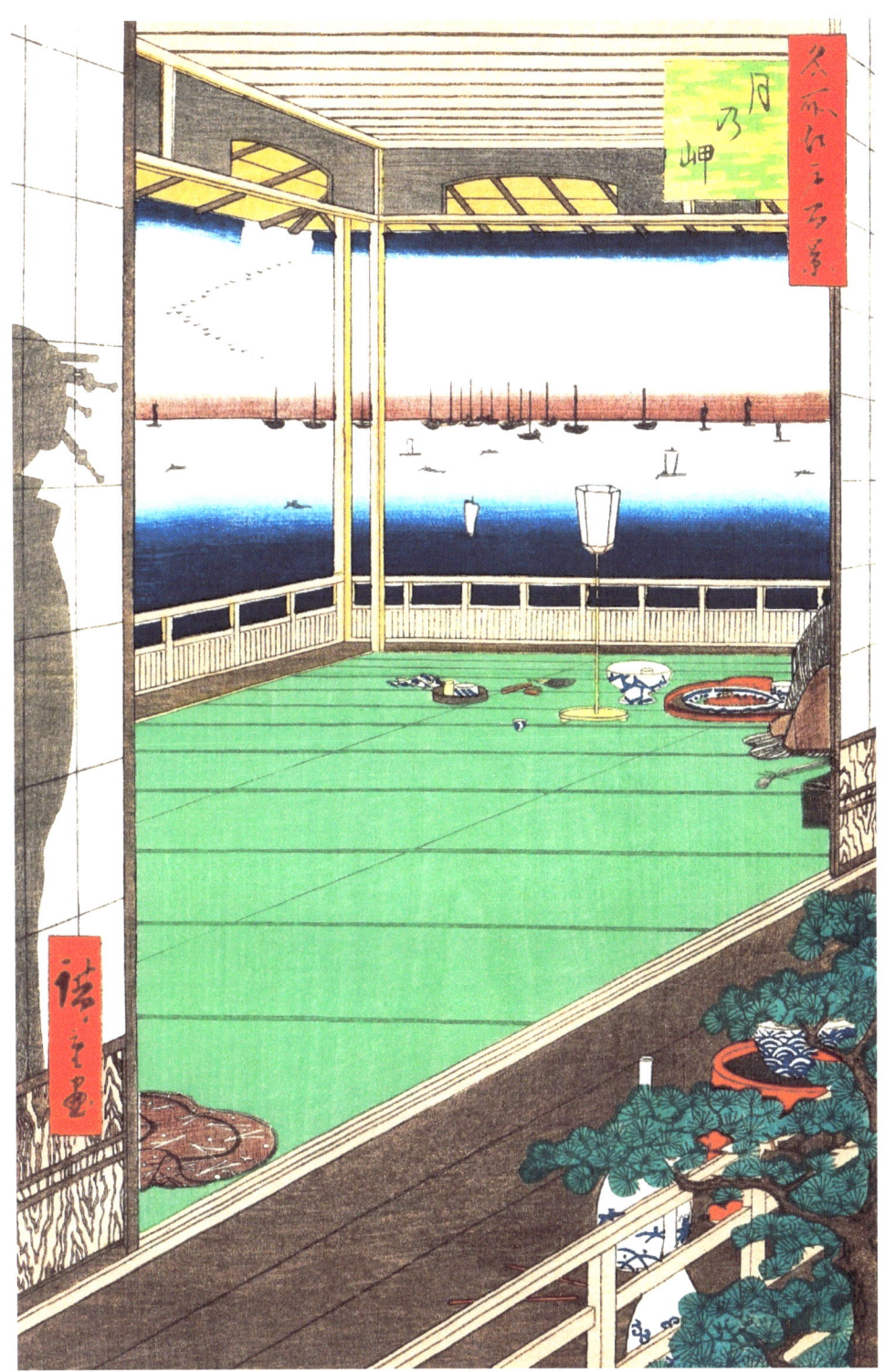

Tsuki no misaki.

The view through two open sliding panels of a porch with large body of water beyond, several boats at anchor beneath a full moon; the shadow of a woman is visible on the left sliding panel and a lamp and eating utensils are at the far end of the porch.

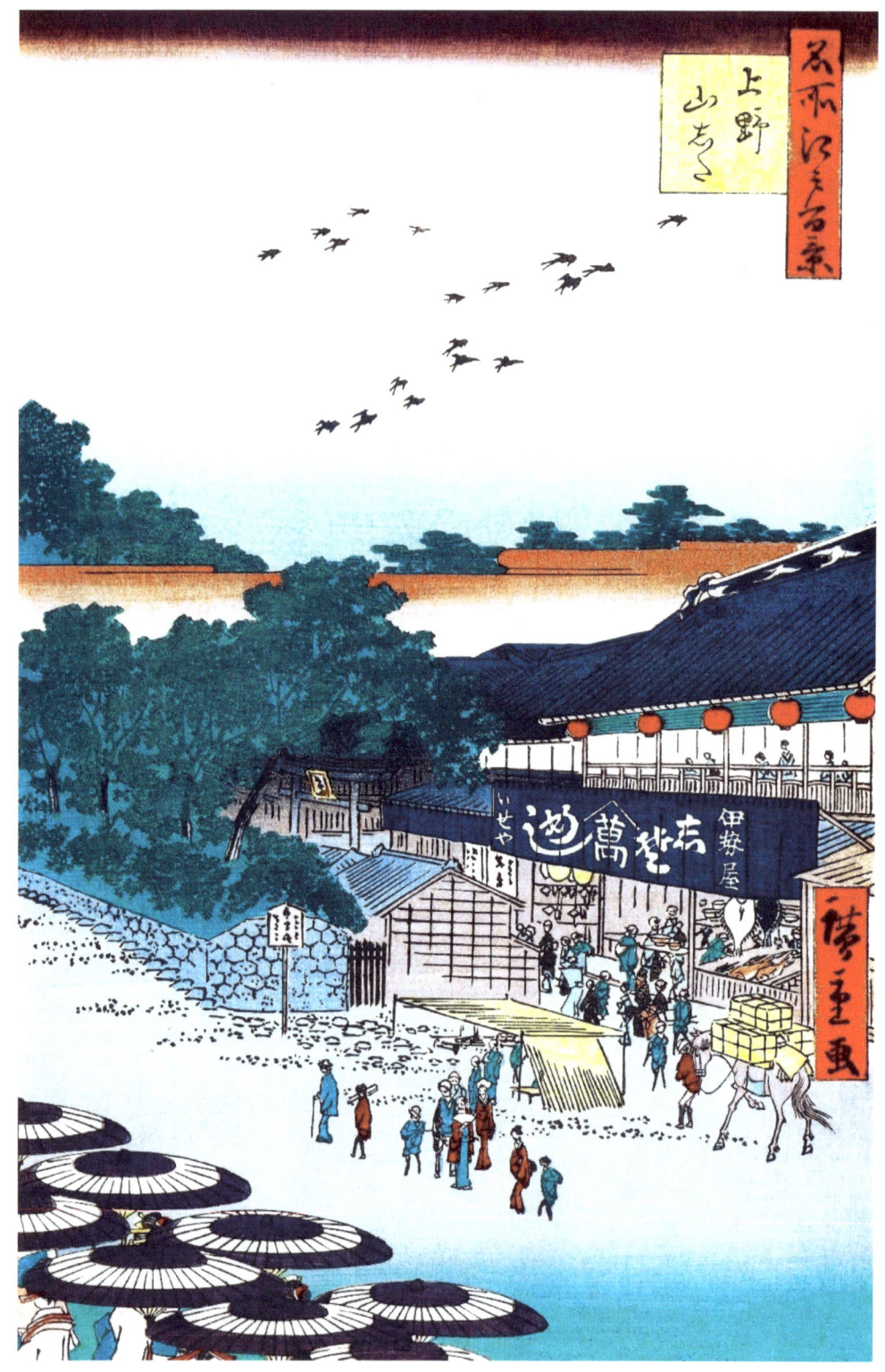

Ueno yamashita.

A bird's-eye view of the Yamashita quarter of Ueno, with the tops of many parasols in the foreground, and travelers and shops in the commercial district.

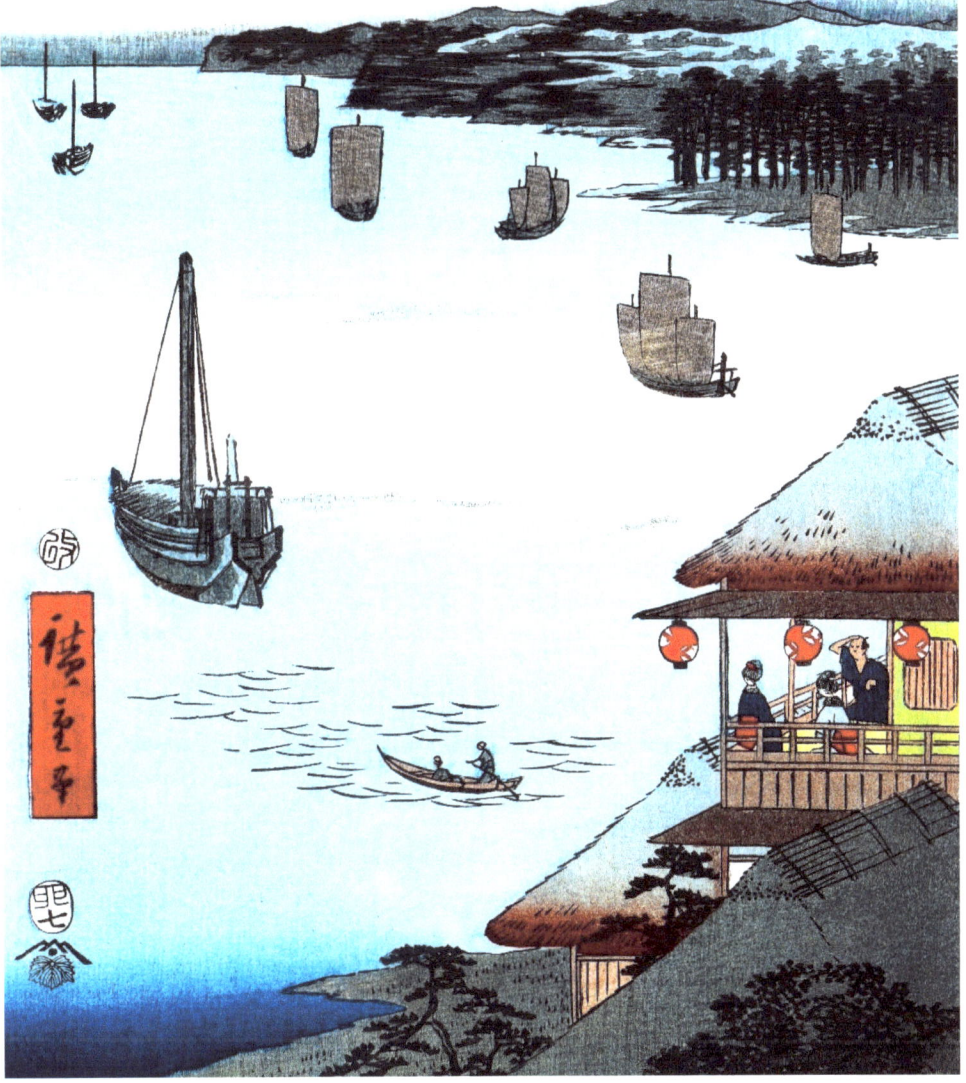

Kanagawa.

A view of ships in a harbor and an inn under a full moon on the coast at the Kanagawa station on the Tōkaidō Road.

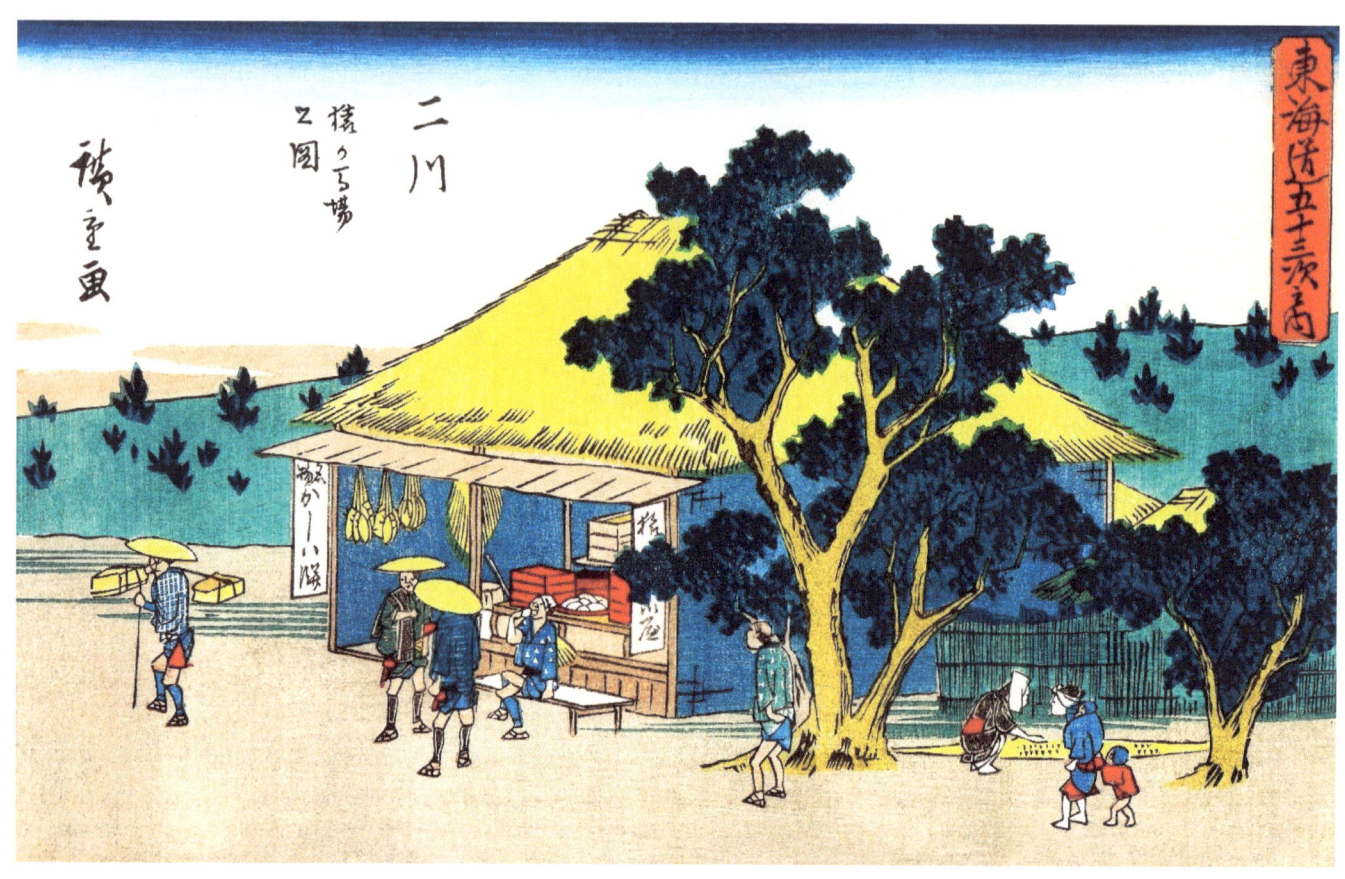

Futagawa.

A man with a shoulder pole, travelers, and others outside a thatched-roof shop, the vendor sitting on a table in front, at the Futagawa station on the Tōkaidō Road.

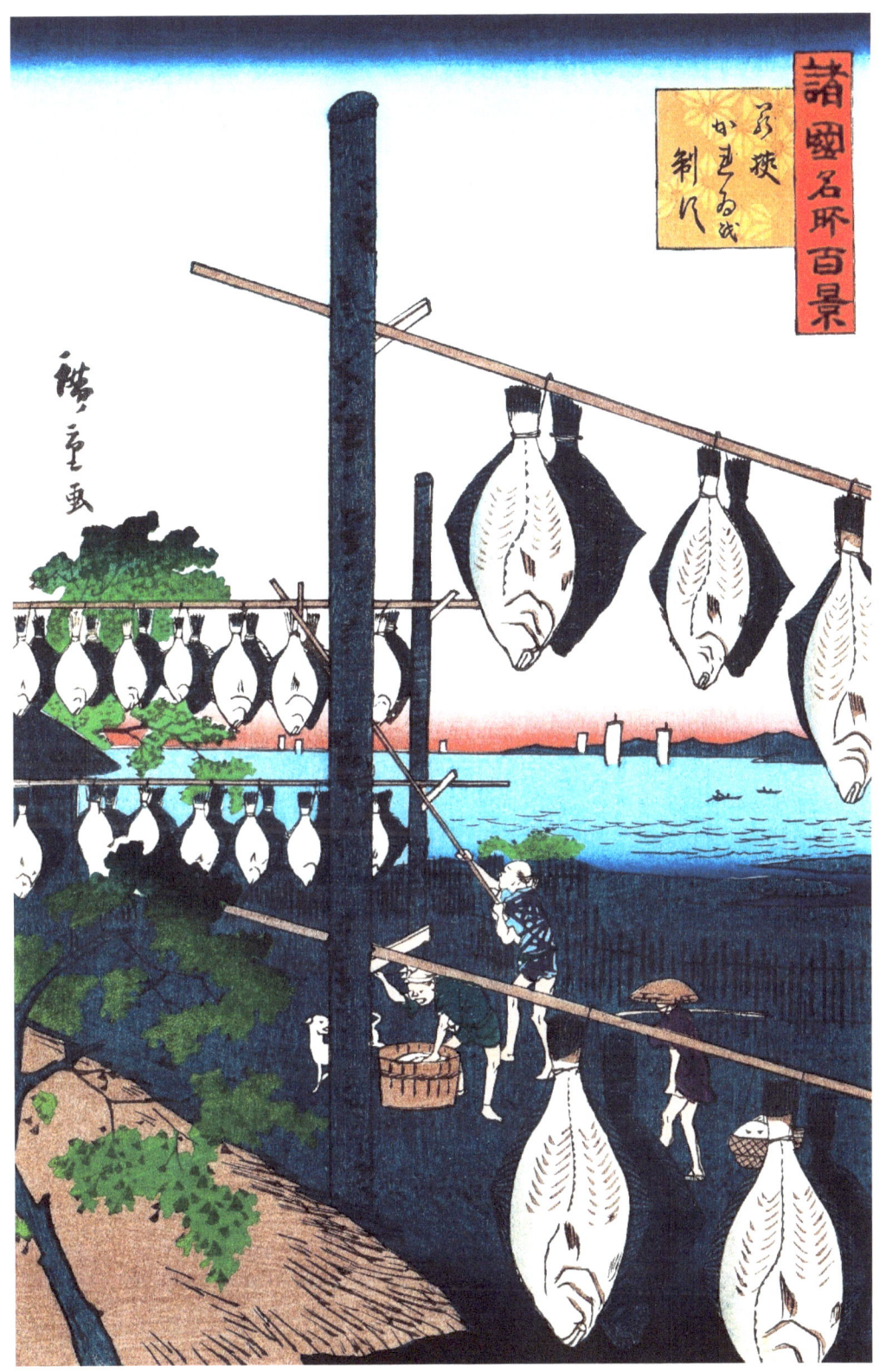

Wakasa karei o seisu.
Fishermen drying flatfish on racks.

www.ingramcontent.com/pod-product-compliance
Lightning Source LLC
Chambersburg PA
CBHW040409220526

45473CB00004B/1182